YO-CUN-836

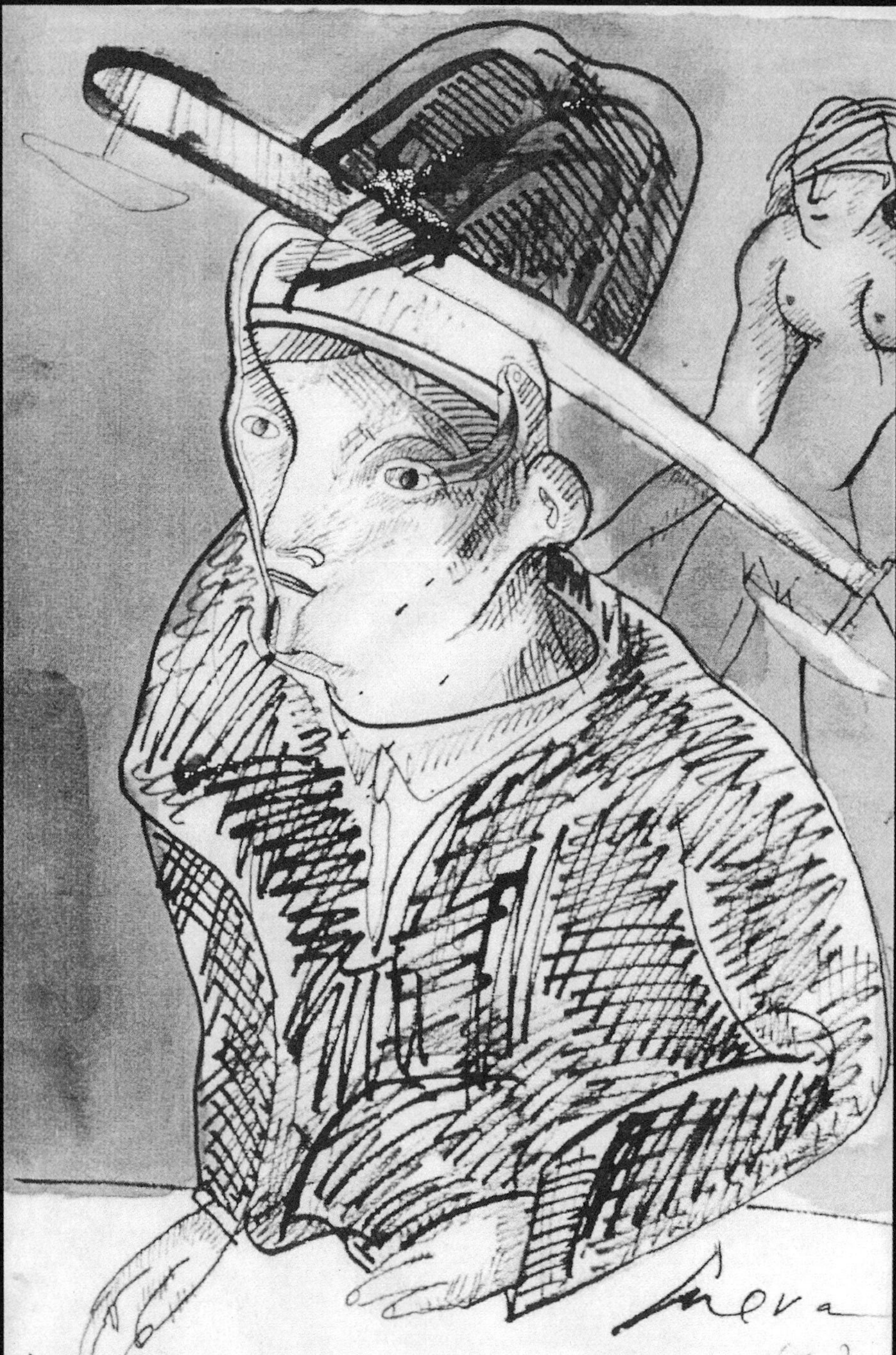

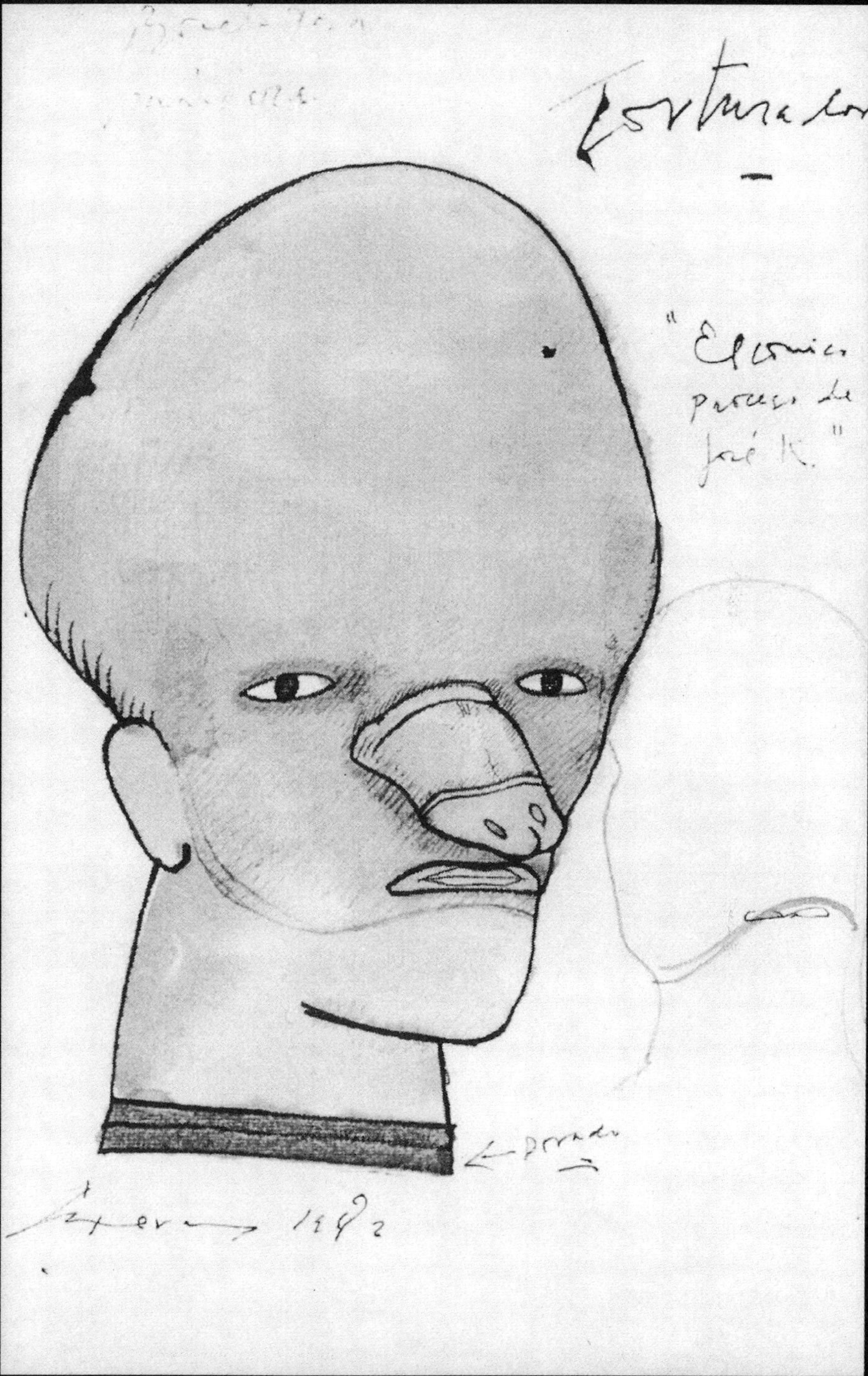
Torturador
"El único proceso de José K."

Figure 1: "José K." José Luis Cuevas, 1982.

the comic trial of text & CONTEXT joseph K.

héctor ortega

edited by manuel flores

1996

SDSU PRESS

the comic trial of text & CONTEXT joseph K.

héctor ortega

edited by manuel flores

SAN DIEGO STATE UNIVERSITY PRESS

Calexico   Mexicali   Tijuana   San Diego

Copyright © 1996 by San Diego State University Press

First published in 1996 by San Diego State University Press,
San Diego State University, 5500 Campanile Drive,
San Diego, California 92182-8141

http://www-rohan.sdsu.edu/dept/press/

All rights reserved.

Except for brief passages quoted in a review, no part of this book may be reproduced in any form, by photostat, microfilm, xerography, or any other means, or incorporated into any information retrieval system, electronic or mechanical, without the written permission of the copyright owners.

Translated from the Spanish by Manuel Flores.

The editor expresses his gratitude for permission to reprint "Quémame no me quemes" (here translated as "Prologue") by Augusto Monterroso.

Originally published in Spanish as
El cómico proceso de José K. (Mexicali: UABC Press, 1995),
The Comic Trial of Joseph K.: Text and Context is published in this first English edition augmented with critical essays by Augusto Monterroso, Héctor Ortega, Hugo Hiriart, Manuel Flores, and D. Emily Hicks.

Front cover photo: "Joseph K. Looking Through a Hole in the Wall" by Rogelio Cuellar.

All photos by Rogelio Cuellar. All drawings by José Luis Cuevas.

Design by Harry Polkinhorn and William Anthony Nericcio

ISBN 1-879691-40-X

9 8 7 6 5 4 3 2 1

PRINTED IN THE UNITED STATES OF AMERICA

CONTENTS

Acknowledgments / x

List of Figures / xiii

Introduction, Harry Polkinhorn / xv

THE COMIC TRIAL OF JOSEPH K. / 1

Critical Essays

    "Prologue," Augusto Monterroso / 71

    "Notes on the Stage Adaptation of Franz Kafka's *The Trial*," Héctor Ortega / 72

    "Héctor Ortega's stage version of Franz Kafka's *The Trial* supposes some kind of equation of syllogisms with three terms," Hugo Hiriart / 84

    "Kafka Unveiled," Manuel Flores / 88

    "Kafka's Humor: The Castle Jester," D. Emily Hicks / 97

Contributors / 115

The Comic Trial of Joseph K. was originally staged at the Santa Catarina Theater, 10 Santa Catarina Plaza (Autonomous National University of Mexico), Coyoacán, Mexico City, in 1982. Cast in order of appearance: Héctor Ortega, David Verduzco, Ramón Barragán, Eduardo Alcántara, Jesús Vargas, Farnesio de Bernal, Estela Chacón, Socorro de la Campa, Emilio del Haro, Mariel Ortiz de Zárate, and Evelin Solares.

Directors
Héctor Ortega/Ricardo Díaz Muñoz

Assistant Director
Manuel Flores Ruiz

Producer
Luis Alberto Ojanguren

Scenography
Francisco Solares

Scenography and Wardrobe
José Luis Cuevas

Original Music
Rafael Elizondo

Lighting Design
Ricardo Díaz Muñoz/Jorge Vértiz

Mural Creation
Sergio Mandujano

Mannequins and Masks
Maricarmen Tostado, Teresa Tostado
Luis Alberto Ojanguren, Leonardo Salas

Recording and Sound Track
Rodolfo Sánchez Alvarado

Technicians
Francisco Solares, Fernando Mendoza
Enrique Montoya, Juan Francisco Solares

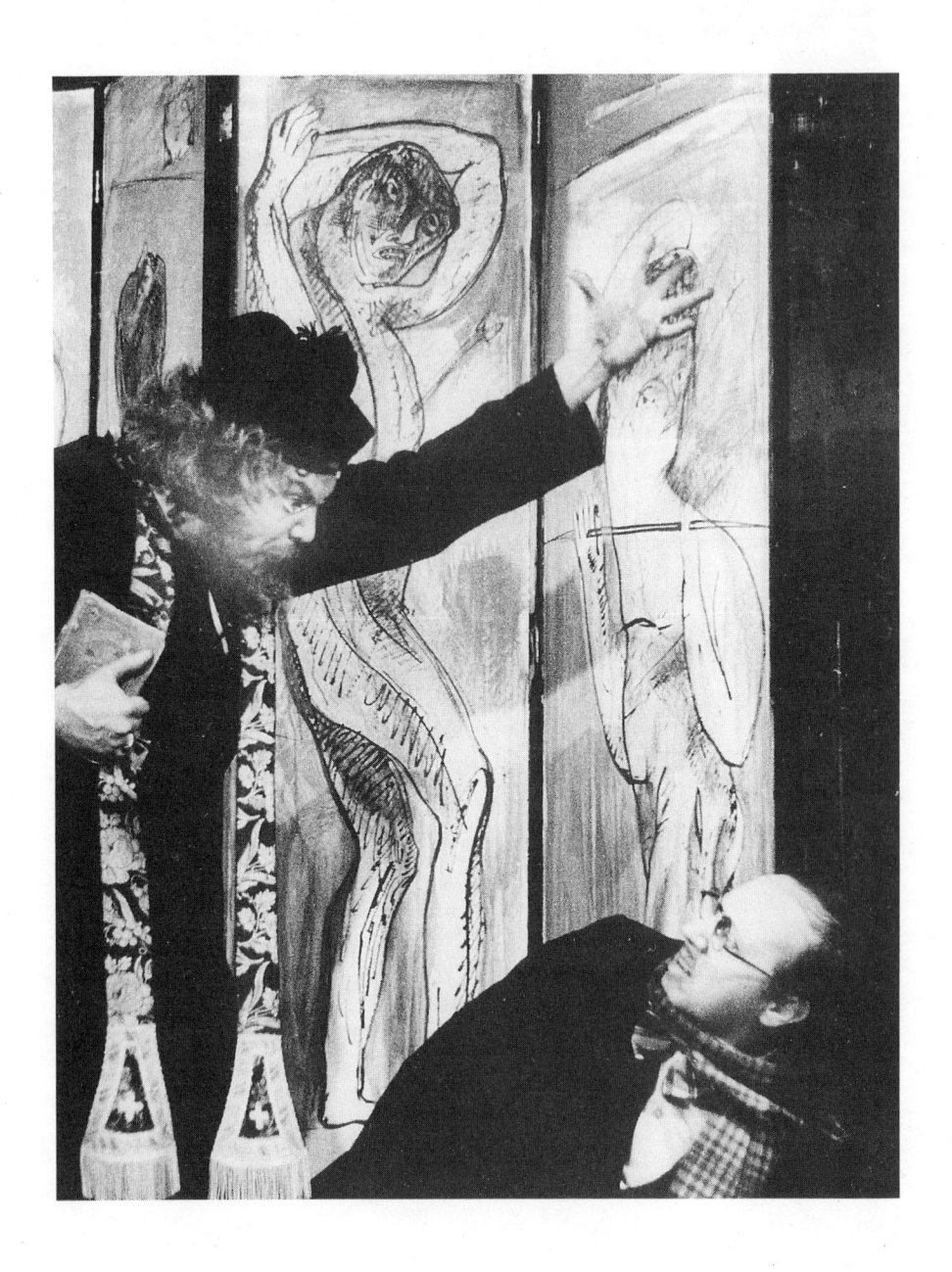

Figure 2. "Before the law stands a doorkeeper."

List of Figures

1. "José K." José Luis Cuevas. 1982. / vi

2. "Before the law stands a doorkeeper." / xii

3. "Judge." José Luis Cuevas. 1982. / xvii

4. "For without having done anything wrong, he was arrested one morning." / xviii

5. "Tinman." José Luis Cuevas. 1982. / 34

6. "I bet this is something organized by my colleagues at the bank because today is my birthday." / 70

7. "Beatle." Augusto Monterroso. / 71

8. "Whipper." José Luis Cuevas. 1982. / 96

9. "Judge of instruction." José Luis Cuevas. 1982. / 118

10. "Office manager." José Luis Cuevas. 1982. / 119

11. "Kullisch." José Luis Cuevas. 1982. / 120

12. "Martyr with impaled hands." José Luis Cuevas. 1982. / 121

13. "Martyr looking up at an angel looking down from a hole in the sky." José Luis Cuevas. 1982. / 122

14. "The lawyer." José Luis Cuevas. 1982. / 123

15. Stage setting for original production. / 124

16. "I'd rather wait for your superior officer." / 125

17. "K. decided to go straight home." / 126

18. "Miss Bürstner, I'd very much like to call you by your first name." / 127

19. "I see him down flat on the floor, surrounded by splashes of blood." / 128

20. "The farther in I go, the worse I feel." / 129

21. "I just broke a plate against the wall to make you come." / 130

22. "Well, if you're innocent, the problem is very simple. But . . . are you innocent?" / 131

23. "Your bad opinion about the way I have conducted myself is because of the soft way you have been treated." / 132

24. "'Like a dog!' said K., before he died." / 133

25. Héctor Ortega, José Luis Cuevas, Ricardo Días Muñoz, Rafael Elizondo, Manuel Flores. Opening night in June, 1982. / 134

26. "That's enough for today; so, we can say good-bye, for now, of course."

Introduction

Harry Polkinhorn

A play script is like a musical score, indications to director and actors guiding their realization of "the play" (different each time). Inherent in drama is the ritualized relationship captured in the binary structure script/performance, transcoded for the adult as play. Contrary to this play, a symbol representing the imagination in its free roaming through the fields at its disposal, is that complex of attitudes and feelings summarized by the term "work," that is, constriction, necessity or fate, Ananke, death. Hence the liberating effect on the viewer of classical tragedy, what Aristotle theorized as catharsis, or purgation through pity and terror. Death is ritually transcended through being confronted.

Kafka of course inverts this formula (just as he inverts so many others). In his fiction necessity displaces imagination. Death is not transcended, but traditional fiction is, through a radical augmentation of the coefficient of the real (here understood as contingency, particularity, specificity, limitation, death). Yet most readers would immediately acknowledge that somehow we remain within the sphere of fiction. Such a perception could only result from an expansion of fiction's range, or an inversion of its manipulations of the culturally embedded imagination/reality ratio. Put otherwise, Kafka takes fiction to a deeper level of the imagination than had been done before, broadening its powers to transform our sense of ourselves and the world.

Central to this historically variable ratio, of course, is character, the most significant device that fiction shares with drama. In the case of both modes of discourse, we are presented with a multiplicity of masks (personae, personalities) that mutually define one another, bring one another into existence, even if these masks or types are seen as comprehended under the implied rubric of a single character. That is, for drama or fiction to exist as such, there must be more than one character, and it is precisely out of the fragmentations of some implied hypothetical meta-character such a situation entails that the other elements of these modes of discourse are generated, especially plot and resolution (or its lack).

Character, then, for example, that of Kafka. Who is he? How can any art escape the straitjacket of identity? Now we see how a bridge has been created between me as viewer/reader and the world of the work of art, always separate but ready to exchange energies with me through masks. Each mask is Janus, two-faced, staring inwards and outwards at the same time. These duplex masks posit space, the non-geometric dimension which the theater represents in the "real" world. The theater (sacred space for transformation of personality) embodies the inescapably and eternally doubled quality of our limited consciousness, pointing around like a beam in the dark yet therefore unable to see behind itself.

To traverse this non-Euclidean space is to unmask character, to strip the personality of its constituent contingency, thereby converting it into another mode of apperception. As Ortega's work demonstrates, Kafka accomplishes this transmutation through humor, the lightning flash that stabs the viewer straight through his or her petrified mask, illuminating for an instant the huge unknown terrain usually cloaked in darkness. Thus it seems natural that Ortega would tease out the humor in Kafka, structured as it is on a fascinatiang series of removes as detailed above. As if to complement these, we see this special problematic reflected in the language complex through which Kafka and Ortega guide us.

Kafka, the Polish Jew living in Prague and writing in German (instead of Yiddish), becomes a symbol for the most extreme of fractured identity politics characterizing our time. *Der Prozes, The Trial, El Proceso, El Cómico proceso de José K., The Comic Trial of Joseph K.;* Yiddish, German, Spanish, and now English. Each translation betrays the original, again repeating the pure guilt and consequent sacrifice visited upon the individual. Humor is the human doorway communicating however imperfectly between levels of this maze.

Figure 3. "Judge." José Luis Cuevas. 1982.

Figure 4. "For without having done anything wrong, he was arrested one morning."

The Comic Trial of Joseph K.

Héctor Ortega

"All Kafka is comic, all Kafka is political."
—Deleuze and Guattari

A two-story stage. From the left- and right-hand side of the spectator, a solid door more or less large, that can sometimes be the door to a church as well as the entrance to the house of the attorney Huld, to the courthouse, and to Joseph K.'s room. A continuation of Joseph K.'s room. A bed, a nightstand, a wardrobe, a small door through which the police agents enter and subsequently take Joseph K. and his uncle into Huld's bedroom. A chaise longe divides the area in two: K.'s office on the right-hand side, which subsequently becomes the place where the judge interrogates K.

When Joseph K. delivers his speech he directs it to the audience in attendance. After this, the area changes into the studio of the painter Titorelli. At the far end, in the center, a door with hangings which where popular in the 1920s. An easel displays a woman in K.'s bedroom, in Huld's house a portrait of the judge, and in Titorelli's studio the drawing which he himself describes: a combination between the Victory of Samothrace and Justice with a blindfold over her eyes and scale. In the church scene, a religious image and a folding screen with martyr pictures.

In K.'s office there is an entrance at the far end. On the right-hand side a coat stand. On the left-hand side, a door with a mirror; it is the stationary room through which the agents promptly exit when they are whipped. On the left-hand side also a spiral staircase.

2   The Comic Trial of Joesph K.

On the upper part, a pulpit where the priest preaches. A window in the back.

K.'s desk, which turns into the judge's instruction chair, now with a chair (made so that the assistant manager can destroy it) in front.

On the upper part, a large mural covers the ceiling of the area where some dolls are sitting; they are the accused. As is described, it gives the impression that there are people sitting, but time has made them appear like beggers.

On the right, a balcony from which the scene of the uncle waiting, soaked, and the hallucinations that Joseph K. has before dying take place. In the back part of the balcony, there are clothes hanged to be dried.

For the upper part, a ladder is required for the actors to climb to the balcony with the clothesline and walk down an aisle with a rail from which the first floor can be seen for the scene where the janitor shows K. the offices.

(*The 1920s. By the balcony area where clothes are hanging to dry, a dark character wearing a black cape and a black chamberga hat like those used by preachers enters through a thick mist. A notable resemblance to a mystery show presented by Orson Welles. The character walks along the high area and descends the spiral stairs. Once down, he addresses the audience in attendance.*)

CHARACTER: (*Solemn and mysterious.*) The essential spirt of bureaucracy is secrecy, the mystery kept in its womb by the hierarchy. If the spirit of the State is known, it appears before the bureaucracy as a betrayal of its mystery. Authority is, therefore, the principle of its existence and the idolatry of authority constitutes its meaning. The State exists only in the form of bureaucratic spirits, whose link is subordination and passive obedience. (*Abandoning solemnity, he takes off his cape, hat, and pants. He's wearing a long night shirt. He gets into bed and goes to sleep, remembers something, and rises to address the public.*) Ah! With regard to the bureaucrat taken individually, he's only interested in placing himself in office; his sole goal is the struggle for the highest positions. (*He lies down and turns off the light. In another light, the narrator enters, a mature man with sloppy beard, wearing a worn out hat and a leather apron; he could be any laborer or craftsman. In each scene he is shown performing a different craft.*)

ACT ONE

NARRATOR: Surely, someone must have been telling lies about Joseph K., for without having done anything wrong he was arrested one fine morning. K. was always used to taking things calmly, but this time Mrs. Grubach, his landlady, failed to bring him breakfast at eight o'clock, which he thought it wouldn't be right to let pass easily. (*K., worried, rises and sits on the edge of the bed. He's surprised. He waits a moment trying to hear something. He reaches to the night table for a bell and rings it. A slim man enters wearing a closely fitting black suit.*)

FRANZ: Did you call?

K: (*Surprised, and covering himself up to his neck with the blanket.*) And who are you? Mrs. Grubach should have brought my breakfast by now! (*Opens the contiguous door and talks to someone evidently standing behind it.*)

FRANZ: (*Mocking.*) He says Mrs. Grubach is to bring him his breakfast. (*He laughs with a contained laugh. From the room next door a guffaw is overheard as an answer. To K.*) No, it won't be possible.

K.: (*Springs out of bed, furious.*) Enough is enough! (*Puts on his pants. K. is wearing a long ridiculous nightshirt.*) I must see what kind of explanation I get from Mrs. Grubach. (*He suddenly stops and repents of his words. He hesitates.*)

FRANZ: Wouldn't you rather stay here?

K.: I don't want to stay here or talk to you until you tell me who you are. (*Opens the door for K., who walks into the contiguous room. A tall and robust man prevents him from stepping out of his room.*)

WILLIAMS: You must stay in your room! Didn't Franz tell you?

FRANZ: You are under arrest. (*K., surprised, recuperates and tries to hide. Pause.*)

K.: But, why?

WILLIAMS: We are not authorized to tell you that. Be patient. You'll be informed at the proper time. (*The warders slap K. on the back. His knees bend. They examine his nightshirt.*) Hum! Nice nightshirt! Did you see?

FRANZ: Beautiful. Elegant. Fine.

WILLIAMS: It's a pity.

FRANZ: You should wear one of less quality.

WILLIAMS: We could take care of the one you have on.

FRANZ: (*Affirms.*) We could even take care of the rest of your underwear, and if the case turns out well we could return it all to you. Right, Willy?

WILLIAMS: It is much better to give these things to us than to leave them at the depot, for in the depot they're usually stolen; after a certain length of time they sell everything regardless of whether the case is settled or not.

FRANZ: And you never know how long these cases last.

K.: I am not interested in your advice. You may dispose of my things as well. Far more important to me is to understand my situation more clearly. Who are you? You surely are police officers. Of course! What else could you be? (*He stops and begins to laugh.*) Ah! How come I didn't think of it before? (*Laughs.*) It was a truly rude joke. (*He claps the warders in a friendly manner to which they do not respond.*) I bet this is something organized by my colleagues at the bank because today is my birthday. I know, the assistant manager? That must be it! (*Laughs freely.*) No? Let me guess. You are the messengers from the store on the street corner whom they have hired for the joke. (*Cries of laughter.*) You look very like it. I, myself, in general, don't like jokes. (*Keeps on laughing.*) The other day, some friends played a joke on me, and I resented them for it. Later on, they complained of me for not taking a joke; so now it won't happen again. This time I'll play along with the joke until the end. (*Stops laughing. The laughing expression on his face freezes.*)

WILLIAMS: (*Rudely.*) For the moment, you're still a free man. (*They separate and leave room for K. to walk towards the door, but at a slight movement of the warders he decides not to and begins looking in his drawers.*)

K.: Allow me, allow me. (*Searches.*)

WILLIAMS: He seems to be a reasonable man. Right, Franz?

K.: What happens is that I am upset. That's why I can't find my identification papers. Ah! Here they are. (*Gives them to the warders.*) My bicycle license. Well, it is true that this is too trivial of a document; but here is my birth certificate. (*The door opens, and Mrs. Grubach shows up carrying a breakfast tray. Franz takes it and places it on the nightstand. Relieved.*) Ah! Mrs. Grubach! Please, come in! (*He turns to the warders who are sitting next to the nightstand devouring his breakfast. They spread butter over the toast dipping it in the creamed coffee. They drink and eat everything except for an apple.*)

WILLIAMS: She is not allowed to because you're under arrest.

K.: I live in a country with a legal constitution where peace reigns and laws are in effect. Here are my identification papers. Now, show me yours and before anything else show me the warrant for my arrest.

WILLIAMS: For God's sake! Don't you realize your situation here? We only want to help you. Right?

FRANZ: Don't be a child. Trust us.

WILLIAMS: What do you want us to do? We're nothing but humble subordinates.

FRANZ: Our officials never go against the people, just like that, searching for crimes; but as the law decrees, the guilty is located first and then we the warders are sent out. That is the law.

K.: I don't know this law.

WILLIAMS: (*Eating.*) All the worse for you.

FRANZ: You see, Willy, he admits his ignorance of the law, and nevertheless, he claims to be innocent.

WILLIAMS: (*Laughing.*) It's of no use to try to reason with him. It's a waste.

K.: Take me to your superiors. A few words with a man of my own level would make everything clearer than hours of chatting with men of plain stupidity.

WILLIAMS: When he orders me, not before. Remember that even if we seem stupid to you, we are at least free men compared to you. And that is no small advantage.

FRANZ: If you have any money, we could bring you a small breakfast from the coffee shop across the street.

K.: For now, I'd rather wait for your superior officer. In the meantime I would like to stay in my room alone for a few moments. (*The warders obey slowly.*) I hope this matter will be settled soon. I wouldn't like to miss work today at the bank. (*Showing off.*) Even so, there's nothing to worry about. Since I hold a high position it would be easily overlooked. I'm the sub-associate director, well, more like the appointed director.

WILLIAMS: (*Holding the door K. is trying to close.*) I suggest you stay calm and wait here for whatever might be decided about you.

FRANZ: Better save your energy because you're going to need it. (*They close the door. K., disturbed, goes to his breakfast. Finds nothing left. Drinks the last coffee. He's hungry; there's only a piece of apple on the tray. He takes a few bites. Turns to the window, yells, and shakes his hand in the air.*)

K.: Shh! What the hell are all those spectators gathering in front of the house for? Get away from there! (*He lies on his bed.*) I can just imagine the attitude of the assistant manager of the bank if I don't show up. What I don't understand is why have those two policemen left me all alone, here where I have so many opportunities to take my own life. What reasons would I have to do so? And why not? (*He goes to the wardrobe and opens it.*) I think a bottle of good brandy is better than a gun. (*He pours the liquor and drinks.*) Only to compensate for the missed breakfast. (*Pours another one.*) And this last one as a precaution before the unlikely possibility that I might need to regain courage. (*They kick open the door. K, almost chokes on the brandy.*)

FRANZ: K.!

K.: What?

FRANZ: The inspector!

K.: At last!

FRANZ: But do you think you can appear before the inspector dressed in your shirt?

K.: Damn it! Leave me alone!

WILLIAMS: He would punish you and us too.

K.: But what do you expect? You come here to arrest me, you drag me out of my bed, and you expect to find me dressed up in my smoking jacket? Stupid formalities! (*He lifts a coat from a chair and shows it to the warders.*) This one? (*They shake their heads.*)

WILLIAMS: You must dress in black.

K.: (*Looks upwards.*) For God's sake! If it helps any in clearing things out. (*The warders search his wardrobe.*)

FRANZ: Fiuuuu! So many suits!

K.: (*Picks one up.*) This is the best coat.

FRANZ: (*Patronizing him.*) The very last fashion!

WILLIAMS: Hmm, American! You must cause a sensation among your acquaintances.

K.: (*Puts his shirt on and gets dressed.*) At least you didn't force me to take a bath.

WILLIAMS: (*Franz leaves.*) Who lives in the room next door?

K.: It's been taken recently by Miss. Bürstner. She's a vulgar typist. She comes home late at night. It's not that I mean to talk badly of her, but she should have more dignity. Up to this month, I have seen her twice walking along on distant streets with a different gentleman each time. (*In response to the warder's gesture.*) You're taking the wrong path. It's not that I feel attracted to her. We have just exchanged a few words in passing. (*While K. talks, Williams places the nightstand in the middle of the room and a chair in a way of a desk. The inspector walks in.*)

INSPECTOR: Joseph K.?

K.: Yes?

INSPECTOR: I suppose you're very much surprised at this morning's events. Am I right? (*He sits on the chair before the nightstand.*)

K.: At last I am before a reasonable man with whom to talk. Certainly, I am surprised but by no means very much surprised.

INSPECTOR: Not very much surprised?

K.: (*Rushes.*) I mean that... (*Tries to find a place to sit down. He can't find one. They're all taken.*) I suppose I can sit down.

INSPECTOR: It's not usual in these cases.

K.: I mean that I am very much surprised, of course, but when one has lived for thirty years in this world and had to find one's way through it, one hardens to surprises and doesn't take them too seriously. Although this lacks importance, the essential thing is to learn who accuses me. Are you officers of the law? None of you wears a uniform.

INSPECTOR: We might wear the most official uniforms and your situation would still remain the same, so don't make such an outcry about your innocence.

K.: Wait a moment! I'm not about to let a younger man than myself come here and lecture me. The lawyer Hasterer is a personal friend of mine; may I call him?

INSPECTOR: I don't see the sense in calling him, unless you have private business to consult with him about.

K.: What sense would there be in calling him when I am under arrest? (*Pretends to call but desists.*) Alright, I won't call him.

INSPECTOR: But, do call him if you want (*Opens the door to let him out.*) Please do telephone.

K.: No, I don't want to now (*Glances through the window.*) Go away! Well, sirs, from the looks of your faces I suppose this affair is over, and since it seems to me that you have nothing better to do than to compare the size of your fingers and to count the amount of matches in my matchbox we might settle this matter and shake hands on it (*Offers his hand to the inspector.*) and get it over with (*The inspector rises and puts on his hat.*)

INSPECTOR: No, my friend, it's not that simple. No, it's not. However, do not fall into despair. You're only under arrest. I was commissioned to inform you and I have, and I have also observed your reactions. That's enough for today. So we can say good-bye, for now, of course. By the way, the fact that you're under arrest doesn't prevent you from leading a normal life.

K.: Ah! Then it means that what I've done isn't so very bad.

INSPECTOR: I never said that it was. In fact, to facilitate your arrival at the bank I detained a colleague of yours so your getting there would be as discreet as possible. (*He enters the scene, brought in by one of the warders, Kullisch, a modest employee from the bank.*)

K.: This pig is not my colleague. He's a low-class employee. I detest him like the rest of them. He's insignificant and will never get promoted in spite of his cringing and repulsive humble humility. I don't see why you have taken such liberties.

INSPECTOR: I only complied with my duty.

K.: A very stupid duty! (*Looks at Kullisch scornfully, who waits looking downwards.*) Well, shall we go to work now? (*They exit. The narrator enters.*)

NARRATOR: For the moment, there wasn't a real reason to worry so much. K. in a short length of time had found his own way to the high position he held in the bank. He had known how to hold on to this position and to command everybody's respect, except for the assistant manager of the bank, who, in spite of hating him and maintaining a continual envy and rivalry against K., always acted as if his relationship with K. were most friendly. The best strategy would be to avoid thinking of his own shortcomings and to hold on to the idea of his superiority.

K.: (*The office space lights up. K. enters, furious. Yells.*) I protest! Yes, I protest! (*He walks toward the utility room. On the inside of one of the doors, there is a large mirror. K. removes his coat and accidentally looks at and appreciates himself. He hangs his coat and hat. The room is full of stationary items, boxes, objects, etc. K. looking at himself in the mirror.*) I protest, your honor! (*He begins* *to imagine how his hearing would be and what he would say to the judge.*) What has happened to me, your honor, is unimportant, and as far as I'm concerned, my case reflects the procedures followed in many others. (*He simulates the sound of a cheering crowd and says Bravo! Bravo!*) Enough! Enough! I do not need unanimous applause. It would be quite pleasing if everyone here considered this particular as I'm not looking for an oratory success. The Examining Magistrate, no doubt, is much a better speaker than I, since it is part of his profession. (*New bravos. As busy as he is with his acting, he doesn't notice that, silently, the assistant manager of the bank has entered and begun searching through K.'s drawers and files. Then he notices the assistant manager's presence. Furious.*) Mr. Assistant manager! What are you doing in my office, searching through my files as if they were your own?

ASSISTANT MANAGER: Oh! Are you there? (*Keeps on searching.*) I'm looking for a copy of the contract that, according to the firm's representative, should be among your papers. Do you want to help me look? (*K. advances towards him.*) Thanks, I found it. (*He carries an enormous pile of papers.*)

K.: Mr. Assistant Manager! You're taking a large amount of documents, obviously not only the copy of the contract. For now, I cannot deal with you because I'm busy with an affair that requires a great deal of delicacy, but I warn you that as soon as my problems are settled you'll regret it, and quite some. (*The assistant manager returns.*)

ASSISTANT MANAGER: You were saying? (*Placing a hand on his forehead.*)

K.: What's wrong with you?

ASSISTANT MANAGER: I have a headache.

K.: I warn you I won't pay any attention to your headache. I intend to settle this once and for all, and I won't be taken in by sentimentality.

ASSISTANT MANAGER: Don't worry. (*He cleans his prescription glasses.*) My headaches are simple; on the other hand, they do not prevent me from thinking.

K.: What do you mean by that? Are you implying that your headaches are different from those I happen to experience and that mine do prevent me from thinking? (*The assistant manager looks around the office with his now clean glasses.*) Take a seat. (*The assistant manager obeys. K. solemnly clears his throat.*) I suppose you're not acquainted with what is happening to me, or you would use it against me ... .

ASSISTANT MANAGER: (*Referring to the chair in which he's sitting.*) Have you noticed that it's loose? (*He begins to fix it, hitting it.*)

K.: Do not interrupt.

ASSISTANT MANAGER: Go on, go on, I'm listening. Don't worry. I can hear and follow perfectly. (*Keeps on fixing the chair.*)

K.: I was telling you that I'm only waiting for the right time to calmly go to your office or invite you to mine to define once and for all our relationship. (*The assistant manager grabs a letter opener. K. gets scared. He thinks he's going to be attacked. The assistant manager only wants to use it as a tool to fix the chair.*)

ASSISTANT MANAGER: May I use your ruler? (*K. searches for one and hands it to him. He uses it as a lever.*) Don't worry. I'm just trying to take it off with the idea of making it fit back into place.

K.: (*Controlling himself.*) It doesn't interest me if the chair has or does not have a defect. Please be kind and leave it alone. And even if it had a defect, what I'm telling you is much more important and more to your benefit than trying to fix it.

ASSISTANT MANAGER: Go on; go on.

K.: I cannot let you go on believing that I'm useless and finished.

ASSISTANT MANAGER: Done! I'm done. (*Hits it with his hand.*)

K.: I need to prove to you that I'm still alive and that like all living creatures I can one day astonish the world with new creative virtues regardless of the little danger that there might be for you at the moment.

ASSISTANT MANAGER: It's tough. Ah! It seems as if only the pressure of my hands is not enough. (*He sits with all his weight on the chair that breaks apart. The assistant manager observes the pieces.*) It's rotten wood. (*K. pushes him out.*)

K.: (*K.'s room lights up.*) Out! Out! (*K. goes on pushing the assistant manager. The narrator enters.*)

NARRATOR: K. had been accustomed to staying in the office until nine. He would take a short walk, alone, or with some of his colleagues, and then go to a beer hall where he would stay until eleven, sitting at a table with some other customers, mostly older than he. Men of eminence, well read, whom K. wanted to be seen with to gain status. Also, once a week K. visited a girl called Elsa, who worked all night as a waitress in a cabaret, and during the day, she would receive her visitors in bed. But on this evening, K. decided to go straight home following his own wish to apologize to Miss

Bürstner for the improper use of her room. (*Narrator exits. K. lies down on the sofa. Gets up and leaves the door to his room slightly open. Lights up a cigar. He lies down for a while and overhears a noise.*)

K.: (*Very interested.*) Miss Bürstner.

MISS BÜRSTNER: Who is calling me? (*Miss Bürstner appears by the door. A girl with curly hair.*)

K.: It's me.

MISS BÜRSTNER: Oh, Mr. K.! Good evening. (*She holds out her hand.*)

K.: I would like to have a few words with you. May I do so now?

MISS BÜRSTNER: Now?

K.: I've been waiting for you. It's not an appropriate time, is it?

MISS BÜRSTNER: Well, as you know I was at the theater, and I had no idea that you were waiting for me.

K.: What I want to talk to you about. It didn't happen until this morning.

MISS BÜRSTNER: I have no objection to listening to you, but I'm so tired that I can hardly stand up.

K.: Come in for a moment. There, in the hall we can't talk because we would wake up everybody, and I wouldn't like that, more for our own sake than for theirs. (*Signals the sofa.*) Sit down; sit down.

MISS BÜRSTNER: (*Stays standing without removing her profusely flowered hat.*) What is it that you have to tell me? I'm quite curious to know.

K.: Well, this morning your room was somewhat messy. In a way it was my fault, and that's why I wanted to apologize.

MISS BÜRSTNER: My room?

K.: Yes.

MISS BÜRSTNER: What happened?

K.: Something horrible. (*Pause. He stares at her.*)

MISS BÜRSTNER: What?

K.: (*Coming back to reality.*) Oh, nothing! I was distracted, contemplating you like that, holding your face on your hand, resting your elbow on the pillow and with the other hand resting on your hip.

MISS BÜRSTNER: (*Self-conscious.*) Well, so far you haven't explained much.

K.: (*Absorbed in her.*) Explain what? Oh, yeah! Should I tell you how things happened?

MISS BÜRSTNER: I'm exhausted.

K.: Well, you came back too late.

MISS BÜRSTNER: Oh, so now you're blaming me! I deserve that! I should have never come into your room. It's all clear that there was no need for that.

K.: Yes, it was necessary. I'll show you. (*He begins to move the furniture as it was.*)

MISS BÜRSTNER: If you think staging is necessary to explain to me ... I warn you that I am so very tired. (*K. sits behind the nightstand as the inspector did.*)

K.: You should picture the places occupied by the various characters. It's something really interesting. I'll do the inspector. There, next to the chest, are sitting two warders. Now the presentation begins. Oh! I forgot the most important character: Me. (*The girl laughs, having fun.*) Well, I'm here, standing before the nightstand. The inspector is sitting comfortably with his legs crossed at his ease, with his arm hanging over the back of the chair like this, ill-mannered. Now the representation begins. The inspector shouts at me, a real scream. (*K. is going to shout. Miss. Bürstner puts her finger to her lips to prevent K. from shouting. Too late.*)

K.: Joseph K.! (*Some knocking from the room next door. K. is startled, as well as Miss Bürstner. He rushes over and seizes her hands.*)

K.: (*Whispering.*) Don't be afraid. I'll put everything right. Who can it be? Nobody sleeps in the next room.

MISS BÜRSTNER: (*Whispering.*) Yes, Mrs. Grubach's nephew sleeps there, since yesterday. He's a captain. You were too absorbed in your role. Why did you have to shout like that? (*Because of the fright they come close together, and K. kisses her on her cheek.*) Don't do that. Let go of me! What are you doing? Don't you see we're been heard through the door? Leave me alone!

K.: No. I won't let you go until you're a little calmer. Let's go. (*He leads her by the hand. She lets herself be lead.*) This incident, though it may be unpleasant for you, is of no importance. You know that Mrs. Grubach adores me and believes anything I say. On top of that, she owes me money. I'll back you up in anything you invent about us being together.

MISS BÜRSTNER: I thank you so very much, but I'm not going to accept. What happened is my responsibility and whatever happens with my life is also only my concern. Now, please let me go. I need to be alone. The few minutes you asked me for a conversation have extended more than they should. (*K. holds her by her hand and then her wrist.*)

K.: You are not angry with me now, are you?

MISS BÜRSTNER: (*She shakes off her hand.*) No, no. I am not angry with anybody. (*K. again takes her by the wrist and leads her to the door. He stops her.*) Let me go! The captain's listening and amusing himself at our expense.

K.: Yes, yes. I'm going to. (*He holds her and kisses her on the lips, then all over her face like a thirsty animal. He ends up with a prolonged kiss on her neck.*)

MISS BÜRSTNER: I'm going. I'm exhausted. (*She leaves and opens the door to her room. K. holds her hand and kisses it.*)

K.: I'm really concerned about you, because of the captain, Miss Bürstner. (*Pause.*) Miss Bürstner, I would like very much to call you by your first name. What is your name? (*The girl slaps him and closes the door, angry.*) Well, I don't know what it is! (*Dark. The narrator enters.*)

NARRATOR: K. was informed by telephone that the next Sunday a short inquiry into his case would take place. Sunday had been selected so K. wouldn't have to interrupt his professional work. Among other things, they specified the location, but they failed to state the time. K. thought that the most convenient time to attend would be at nine a.m., since that was the time at which tribunals start during work days. Thinking about the closeness of the relation between law and crime, he walked up a staircase chosen at random. His real search began on the first floor. And since he couldn't ask directly for the Court of Inquiry, he invented a supposed carpenter named Lanz and began asking after his residence. So he called at the first door he found. (*Knocking is heard. The narrator exits. A woman of sparkling black eyes, with a bucket of wet baby clothes, opens the main door. K. shows up. In this scene, we discover a gallery on the second floor, in which men and women await bent under the low ceiling. A bold sign reads "Generally our trials have foregone conclusions."*)

K.: Excuse me. Does a carpenter named Lanz live here?

WOMAN: Come in, please.

K.: Perhaps, you have misunderstood my words. I've asked you for a carpenter, a man named Lanz.

WOMAN: I know. Come through; come in. I must close this door after you. Nobody else must come in.

K.: This seems like a political meeting. Very reasonable. There is enough people in the room and too much smoke and dust. (*Looking at the public.*) For what it seems, they appear to be divided in two groups. Or perhaps in three, because all those men from the gallery seem to be dressed worse than the people below. I wonder what it is that I should say to win the whole audience. Or if that isn't possible, at least the majority.

WOMAN: Come along. Come. (*She leads him to the opposite extreme of the room, where, on top of a platform, they have placed a table. Behind it, almost at the edge of the platform, there is a man sitting. He is rude and short, and when he talks he does so with* merriment and gasping. *The man writes in a well-worn school notebook. He wears a long, old, black coat that fits him loosely. He carries a badge on his collar. The woman leaves K. before the judge, who doesn't look at him for a long while. K. tries on several occasions to call his attention. Finally, the judge looks at K,. brings out his watch and with a penetrating look addresses him.*)

JUDGE: You should have been here an hour and five minutes ago. (*During the interrogation there is a murmuring noise that can be heard, approving or disapproving, as well as pre-recorded laughs. The men from the gallery are well dressed puppets, with expensive clothing that time has eaten. When the judge reprimands K. for his delay, the murmuring grows louder and decreases.*)

K.: Late or not, I am here.

JUDGE: Yes, but now I am not obligated to hear you. Nevertheless, I will make an exception today; but I warn you that another delay shall not occur. Now, step to the platform. (*K. obeys. The judge examines the registration notebook.*) So, you are a house painter?

K.: No, I am the sub-associate director of an important bank.

JUDGE: (*Indignant.*) Quiet! Quiet!

K.: And that question of yours, Sir, about my being a house painter — although more than a question, you simply made a statement to that effect. It defines clearly the way of these proceedings in the trial against me. There is no doubt that behind the diligent works of justice, there is an important organization at work that not only employs corrupt agents, idiot inspectors, and mediocre judges, but it also relies on a whole judicial machinery of servants, policemen, and other assistants and most assuredly even executioners, and I'm not taking back my word, gentlemen. I would love to see those depots where the goods, acquired with great effort by arrested men, are left to rot only after the thieving officials have helped themselves. (*He stops. Looks at the audience. Through the main entrance the washerwoman enters, now without the bucket. K. is distracted from his speech. The judge sits down and thumbs through his notebook. K. grabs it from the judge's hands.*) Your own notebook, Sir, confirms my suspicion. (*He lifts it up high to show it; he handles it with his finger tips and with disgust.*) These are the records of the examining magistrate, a worn-out and greasy school notebook. (*He tosses it over the table. K.'s speech is interrupted by a shriek from the washer woman who is now in the corner coddling with a young man. K. peers from beneath his hand trying to see what is taking place in that corner. More yelling from the man is overheard. K. turns aggressively towards the couple.*) Isn't there anyone who can eject this couple from the hearing? It seems to me, Sirs, from the first rows, that you are not only impassive but delighted with the disturbance of the seriousness I've introduced into this gathering. I see that my speech has caused no effect upon you. You have been disguising your real opinions while I spoke. And now at the end of my speech you take your masks off. (*K. addresses the judge.*) Oh! So you also wear that badge beneath your beard. (*Staring at the man's collar. Turns to the public.*) You all wear on your lapels badges of different shapes and colors, but you're all accomplices. You pretended to gather in groups of different opinions to lead me on. I hope you have amused yourselves, thinking that I innocently thought you would come out to defend innocence. (*He walks towards the door. The woman tries to stop him in good will.*) Step aside, or I'll punch you! (*Takes his hat and walks to the exit in a great silence.*)

JUDGE: Just a moment! I warn you that as of now you have flung away all the advantages which your interrogation might have conferred on you. (*K. laughs loudly.*)

K.: You scoundrels. (*Opens and exits.*) Keep your interrogations!

The Comic Trial of Joesph K.

(*Music. Lights dim.*)

NARRATOR: During the following week, K. waited for a new summons. He couldn't believe that his refusal to be interrogated had been taken seriously, and since by Saturday afternoon he had not received any, he assumed that he was supposed to attend again on Sunday at the same hour. This time he didn't have to make any inquiries, and he went straight to the hearing room. (*Exits. The washer woman opens the door.*)

WOMAN: There is no sitting today.

K.: What do you mean there's no sitting?

WOMAN: No, there isn't. The room is empty. If you don't believe me . . .

K.: May I glance at those books? It's not that I'm curious, but at least my coming here will not be pointless.

WOMAN: No, it isn't allowed; those books belong to the Examining Magistrate. (*Closes the door.*)

K.: Hum! I see. Evidently those are law books from which an essential part of the justice dispensed here comes. (*Reads out loud a sign that says "NOT ONLY IS IGNORANCE OF THE LAW CONDEMNED, BUT SO IS INNOCENCE".*)

WOMAN: Well, I don't understand quite well, but I think that's how it goes.

K.: Well, then I shall go.

WOMAN: Do you want me to give the Examining Magistrate a message?

K.: Do you know him?

WOMAN: Of course. My husband is an usher. They give us free shelter here.

K.: That doesn't surprise me at the least, but to learn that you are married . . .

WOMAN: Do you mean, because of what happened during the last meeting when I caused a disturbance while you were talking?

K.: Yes, that's what I mean.

WOMAN: All the better for you, because from what I heard, you caused a bad enough impression.

K.: That doesn't excuse you!

WOMAN: I am excused by all those who know me. The man who was embracing me on Sunday has been after me for a long time. Perhaps to most men I may not be seductive, *per se*, but I am to him. Oh! I can't find the way to get rid of him! My husband has grown to accept the situation, since that young man is a student and will probably rise to a high position. (*She fixes her dress and her hairdo.*)

K.: It wouldn't surprise me. He's perfectly adapted to all that happens here.

WOMAN: You're anxious to change things here, aren't you? That's my impression from your speech. I liked it a lot. Well, at least, what I heard of it. Oh, this is horrible! (*Takes K.'s hand.*) Do you think you'll make an improvement around here? (*K. smiles petulantly, caressing the woman's hand.*)

K.: Well, the truth is that the need to reform this machinery of justice never made me lose any sleep, but the fact of being under arrest forces me to intervene in all this to protect my own interests, and if at the same time I may be of any help, I'd do it gladly. You could also help me.

WOMAN: In what way?

K.: By showing me the books on the table, for instance.

WOMAN: Of course! (*She invites him to follow her.*)

K.: (*Looking at the books.*) Hum! They're quite old and maltreated. How dirty everything here is! (*With the tip of her apron, the woman dusts the books. K. takes one of the books gingerly, opens it, and closes it rapidly.*)

WOMAN: What happened?

K.: Nothing. There is an indecent picture. A man and a woman sitting on a couch. The intention of the draftsman is evidently obscene. He didn't come but with a couple of figures, ugly and with no perspective. (*The woman tries to see, but K. does not allow her. Takes a book and opens it on the title page.*) It seems to be a novel. *How the perverted Snow White tormented her seven dwarf husbands.* And these are the law books that are studied here! These are the men who are supposed to judge me?

WOMAN: I'll help you. I'm not afraid of danger. I only feel afraid when I want to. (*She sits on the edge of the platform and leaves room for K. next to her.*) You have beautiful black eyes. I've been told that I also have pretty eyes, but yours are much more lovelier.

K.: It is always the same thing. You're offering yourself to me.

You're as corrupt as the rest of them. You're so sick of all the officials here that you become excited over any stranger. That's why you are complimenting my eyes. (*Rises.*) I don't believe you can help me. I'm sure you only know subaltern officials whom I don't think would have any influence over the final result of my trial. I'm sorry to talk to you like this, and, to return some of your compliments, I must confess that I am attracted to you, too. Especially when you gaze with such sorrowful eyes like you're doing now. On the other hand, I see no reason for it.

WOMAN: (*Holding K.'s hand.*) No! You can't go now. You can't leave with a wrong idea of me.

K.: (*Sits again.*) You have not understood me. If you really want me to stay I'll stay, gladly. My words had no other meaning than to beg you not to do anything for me in these proceedings. Yes, you can do something for me. You may inform the judge that nothing will induce me to bribe these officials even if they use all the artifices in which undoubtedly they are ingenious. You can tell them they're wasting their time. (*Interested.*) By the way, do you really know the Examining Magistrate?

WOMAN: Of course! And from what I can tell, he is interested in me. Yesterday, through the student, he sent me a pair of silk stockings as a reward for cleaning the courtroom. Look; they're really fine quality. (*Lifts her skirt provocatively.*) I would say too fine for a woman like me. (*Suddenly she interrupts her talking and puts her hand on K.'s hand.*) Shh! Bertold is watching us. (*By the door, there is a man standing, short and bow-legged, with a short, reddish, and abundant beard that he keeps caressing.*)

K.: Hmm! It's the first time that I've come across a student of this mysterious judicial science. (*Bertold makes a sign to the woman without paying any notice to K. He goes to the window and waits.*)

WOMAN: Don't be angry with me, and don't think badly of me, but now I have to go to that horrible creature. I'll be back in a minute, and then I'll go with you wherever you want and you can do with me anything you please. I'd like to get away from here, forever. (*Presses K.'s hand against her and leaves towards the student.*)

K.: (*Trying to stop her.*) Wait! (*The woman leaves. K. stays, pacing up and down, trying to make as much noise as possible. He goes to the table and begins hitting it with his knuckles, his hands, and finally with his fists. The student has been steadily muttering something incomprehensible to the woman while embracing her and kissing her. She lets him have his way with her, although at times she rejects him. Bertold turns to K.*)

BERTOLD: (*Student.*) If you're so impatient, you can leave. Get lost! Nothing prevents you from going. No one will miss you.

K.: I am impatient, it's true, and the easiest way to relieve my impatience would be for you to leave us alone. And, although I'm not very well versed in the legal training, I suspect that it's not about learning how to make rude remarks, at which you seem to have attained a great deal of perfection.

BERTOLD: I told the Examining Magistrate from the very beginning. It was a mistake. They shouldn't let you free.

K.: Enough of conversation. (*Takes the woman by the hand.*) I like this woman. Come with me.

BERTOLD: Ah! That's it? (*They begin pulling her.*) Ah, no! You're not taking her! (*Bertold lifts the woman over his shoulder and runs towards the door. To make K. mad, he caresses her arm. K. runs after him.*)

K.: Don't go away. Don't be scared. I'm not going to strangle you, although I'd like to.

WOMAN: Don't try to do it. The Examining Magistrate has sent for me. I don't dare go with you. This little monster wouldn't let me go.

K.: But, don't you want to be free? (*Lays his hand over the student's shoulder, and he bites it.*) Ouch!

WOMAN: No, you shouldn't be doing this. What are you thinking of?! It would be my ruin. Let him go, please!

K.: Fine, then go away! I don't want to ever see you again! (*He punches the student on the back, who stumbles and exits happily at having won. K. kicks the door. The woman waves her hand and shrugs her shoulders.*) Bow-legged student, insignificant, lofty bearded student!

NARRATOR: K. recognized that this was his first defeat those people had visited upon him; Nevertheless, how well off K. felt in comparison to the Examining Magistrate who had to sit in a garret, while K. had, at the bank, a large room with a waiting room next to it, from which he could see the busy life of the city through the enormous fine glass windows! True, he didn't enjoy a secondary income from bribes or frauds and couldn't order his secretary to bring him a woman to his office but . . . (*The usher enters. An old man in civilian clothes, who, as a professional emblem, carries attached to his jacket two golden buttons that looks as if they had been stripped from an old army coat.*)

USHER: Excuse me. Have you seen a woman around here?

K.: You're the usher, right?

28   *The Comic Trial of Joesph K.*

USHER: Yes. Oh! You are the defendant K. Now I recognize you. Welcome. *(He holds out his hand. K. doesn't correspond.)*

K.: I spoke with your wife just a moment ago. In fact, the student took her up to the Examining Magistrate.

USHER: Ah! You see, Sir. He always takes her away from me. Even on a Sunday, like today. I'm not supposed to work today, but they sent me to do useless errands just to keep me away from here. And they make sure not to send me too far away so I can be back in minutes if I hurry. I go running, as fast as I can; from the half opened door of the office, I go; I yell the message, nearly breathless, so they hardly understand me, and I come back at full speed. *(Mimicking himself.)* And yet, the student always gets here before I do. And of course his way here is much shorter. He only has to come down the staircase from the attic. If it weren't because I'd risk my job, I would have squashed him against the wall a long time ago. *(Imagining.)* I see him down flat on the floor, squashed, arms spread, fingers separated, legs twisted and surrounded by splashes of blood. *(Sighs.)* But so far it's only been a dream. And things are turning even worse. Up until now, he used to take her for his own pleasure, but now he's taking her to the Examining Magistrate.

K.: *(Jealous.)* Well, isn't your woman responsible for any of this?

USHER: Of course she is. She's to blame the most. She was the one who offered herself to him. As for him, he runs after every woman he sees. Unfortunately, my wife is the most beautiful one of the neighborhood, and I am not in a position to defend myself.

K.: By the way you're saying it, there is nothing to be done, it seems.

USHER: And why not? It would only take a good thrashing one of those times when he's chasing my wife. He would not do it ever again because he is a coward by birth. But I can't do that, and I don't have anyone to ask that favor of. They're afraid of him. He's very influential. Only a man like you could do it.

K.: And why a man like me?

USHER: Because you're under arrest, aren't you?

K.: All the worse for me. I could influence my interrogation, although that doesn't mean that I can't take the student on my account.

USHER: I would be so very grateful to you.

K.: Perhaps some more officials here, even all of them, deserve such just treatment.

USHER: (*Laughing.*) Yes, indeed. (*Calls him, confidentially.*) Just between us, everyone is rebellious. (*Stops the conversation.*) Now, I must report upstairs. Would you like to come along?

K.: Is there anything interesting to see?

USHER: You can look around in the offices. No one would pay any attention to you.

K: (*Interested*) O.K., I'll come with you. (*K. runs more quickly than the usher, tries to go up the stairs, stumbles.*) These people don't show much consideration for the public. I almost fell on this step.

USHER: They have no consideration whatsoever. And you'll

see the waiting room. (*They go out through the stairs. At the end, the narrator enters the gallery-hallway on the top floor. The moppets sitting on the gallery are grotesque rich people. The narrator enters.*)

NARRATOR: They walk through sordid hallways, without any light or windows. In general, everything is dirty, worn out, and truly depressing.

USHER: (*Referring to the moppets.*) Some time ago, all these people used to have the appearance of decency and good education. (*The moppets sitting along the wooden bench.*)

K.: In spite of their careless dress, it is obvious that they belong to the highest class of society. Nevertheless, they give the impression of street beggars. Hurry up! It bothers me to be walking a few steps ahead of you in a place like this. I may give the impression of a prisoner under guard. (*Stops and looks at the moppets.*) How many humiliations must these people have suffered!

USHER: Yes, they're accused men. All these people are waiting for the final outcome of their trials.

K.: Oh, really? Ah! Then, they're colleagues of mine. (*Miss Bürstner, dressed as a bullfighter with a cape, walks down the hall, or may be spotted through a special light.*) Look, that must be a foreigner. How colorful what the foreign countries have to offer! (*To one of the moppets.*) Excuse me. What are you doing here? I'm also under arrest, but as true as I stand here, I haven't given testimony nor do I intend to do so. Do you consider that necessary? (*Pulls one of the moppets rudely.*) Answer me! Answer me!

USHER: Be careful. Most accused men are very touchy. (*On the lower floor, a man in uniform enters along with a girl.*)

MALE FRONT DESK EMPLOYEE: Mr. Usher, what is going on? Is there a problem?

USHER: No, no, nothing, Sir. Everything is in order.

K.: Well, I have seen all this horror. How do I find the door out? There are so many hallways here that I'll never find my way out.

USHER: Don't shout like that!

FEMALE DESK EMPLOYEE: May I help you gentlemen?

K.: (*To the usher*) You see, you assured me that no one would pay any attention to me, and now how do I tell them that I'm here because I wanted to know if this system of justice is as loathsome inside as it is on the outside? And from what I have seen I'm quite depre1ssed. I need to get out of here. (*K. gets dizzy and almost falls on the staircase. Both employees help him to a chair. The usher exits.*)

GIRL: (*Cheerfully kind as if she were a tourist guide or a flight attendant.*) Would you like to sit down? You feel a little dizzy, don't you? (*Pause.*) Don't worry. Almost everyone suffers an attack of this kind the first time they come here. It is your first visit, right? (*K. nods.*) You see. Here the sun beats down on the roof beams, which makes the air stuffy and unbreatheable. And on top of this add the fact that washing of all kinds is hanged out here to dry. No wonder you feel a little dizzy. When you have returned two or three times, you won't notice it as much. Feeling better?

K.: No, no, I'm sorry! I thank you for your explanation, but it turns out that now that I know the cause of my faintness, I don't feel better. I feel worse.

GIRL: *(Takes a stick with a hook.)* Don't worry. I'll open this little skylight to let in some fresh air. *(The skylight is located right over K.'s head. When it's opened, so much dust falls that K. is covered. The girl has to close it back up and clean K.'s hands with her handkerchief.)* You can't stay here. We're in the way. If you wish, I'll take you to the infirmary.

K.: No, no, not to the infirmary. The farther in I go, the worse I feel. No, I think I'm able to leave now. *(He gets up, his legs shake, he sits back down.)* Well, it seems I can't. *(Employee dressed in an elegant uniform with a nice gray vest talks to K.)*

MAN: I think the gentleman's faintness is due to the atmosphere around here, for which I think the best thing we can do is take him to the exit and not to the infirmary.

K.: *(Delighted.)* Yes, yes, that. I'm sure I'll feel better. I usually don't suffer these kinds of attacks. I'm also an official, and so I'm used to the bad air in offices, but as you have said, this air here is more than I can bear. *(He lifts his shoulders to be taken by the arms. The man ignores him and laughs as he sticks his hands in his pockets.)*

MAN: *(To the girl.)* You see, I was right. This gentleman only feels sick here, and nothing happens to him outside. *(The girl calls his attention by tapping the man on the arm.)* Calm down. Of course I'm going to show the gentleman to the exit. Gosh, this is just what I needed.

GIRL: Don't pay any attention to him, Sir. He's always joshing. This gentleman represents our information bureau. Since our procedures are not well known to the populace, there are a lot of inquiries. See for yourself the way he dresses. We, the employees, thought that since he continually deals with the clients, and he's the first one they have to talk to, well, he should dress with elegance, right? As for us, we're badly dressed and old fashioned. Of course it wouldn't make sense for us to spend our money on clothes since most of the time we're here in the offices. We even sleep here. And since the administration has some peculiar ideas about this matter, it doesn't want to finance the expenses, so we opened a collection to which some clients contributed, and with that money we bought him this nice suit and some others for him to have an excellent appearance. But he spoils it all with his loud laughing, which scares people off.

MAN: That's right, but I don't understand why you are telling this gentleman all of our secrets. He doesn't even care. Just look at his face. (*Looks at K. totally absorbed in his own thoughts. They pick him up by the shoulders.*) Up you go. Courage, you weakling.

K.: Many thanks to both of you. (*Trying to smile. They get to the door. The man opens, and K. stands still trembling before her.*)

MAN: (*Laughing.*) Ha! First he says he wants to go, and now, at the door, he doesn't want to go. (*K. reacts, and before he leaves he takes a small mirror, gives it to the girl, and he combs his hair. He shakes their hands several times.*)

K.: Many thanks, thanks, thanks. Oh, I'm sorry for keeping you next to the exit door. Accustomed as you are to the office air, the relatively fresh air from the stairway must make you ill. (*After saying this, the man feels dizzy now. K. holds them and takes them inside. K. feels dizzy. The employees take him out. Same game. K. exits rapidly and closes the door... The narrator enters and holds the employees to prevent them from fainting, takes them from the stage.*)

END OF FIRST ACT

Figure 5. "Tinman." José Luis Cuevas. 1982.

ACT TWO

NARRATOR: The next day, K. stayed late talking business with the bank director, who showed his concern for K.'s future. Certainly, by ,investing just a few minutes of his time the director used that concern as just a stratagem to earn the appreciation of his employees, as well as their efforts developed over the years. In any case, K. felt conquered once again. He was about to leave when he heard a noise in the utility room. (*Narrator exits. K. enters his office; takes his hat and coat from the perch; hears a noise coming from the utility room. He opens it to see himself in the mirror. In the small room, instead of the office supplies that we saw in the previous scene, there are three men. One of them is dressed in a black leather outfit that leaves his neck, chest, and arms totally bare. He is flogging the agents Franz and Williams with a rod.*)

WILLIAMS: Sir!

FRANZ: We're being flogged because you complained about us, before the Examining Magistrate.

K.: What? I didn't complain. I just told him what happened in my room. And after all, your behavior was much to blame.

WILLIAMS: (*Franz takes cover behind Williams to avoid being flogged.*) Sir, if you only knew how badly paid we are, you wouldn't be as hard on us.

FRANZ: Yes, I want to get married, and he has a family to support. Your fine shirts were a temptation. You are right when you say that it's forbidden to us warders to behave the way we did. It was a mistake, but it is almost a tradition that the underwear be confiscated by the warders. It's always been like that. Believe me.

K.: I never asked for you to be punished. I only intended to defend a matter of principle.

FRANZ: Aayy! (*He's hit. To K.*) We are agents proud of our duties. You must admit that we guarded you quite well.

WILLIAMS: We had a whole career ahead of us. We would have been promoted to a first class whipper like this man. But we have lost everything now. (*They cry.*) And if that wasn't enough, we're being whipped and for us warders it is terribly embarrassing.

K.: (*Asking the whipper for his rod.*) May I? (*Whipper lets him have it.*) Can this rod cause such terrible pain? (*K. waves the rod violently to test it and unwillingly hits Franz, who convulses in pain. K., embarrassed, apologizes and turns to the whipper.*) Thanks. Isn't there any other way to punish these men than to flog them?

WHIPPER: No! (*Smiles and shakes his head.*) Undress! (*To K.*) You mustn't believe what they say. All this man says about his career is a lie. Just look how fat he is. Do you know where that fat comes from? It comes from eating the breakfasts of all the men he has arrested. Didn't he eat yours? There you have it. Such a glutton could never become a good whipper.

WILLIAMS: Well, but there are some chubby whippers like myself.

WHIPPER: (*Whips him.*) Shut up!

K.: Ok, ok. Look, I'll reward you well if you overlook this. Ah? What do you say? (*Pulls out his wallet.*)

WHIPPER: Ah! So now you want to file a complaint against me, so I'll also get whipped?

K.: Be reasonable. If I had wanted to have these men punished, I wouldn't be offering you money to let them go. From my point of view, I don't consider them guilty. The guilt lies within the system. The real guilty ones are the high officials.

FRANZ: Yes, yes!

WILLIAMS: That's right! (*They're beaten.*)

FRANZ: If you can't get us both spared, at least try to get me off. Willy is older than I. His skin is far less sensitive. My poor girlfriend is waiting for me at the door of the bank. I feel so ashamed and miserable! (*Cries and dries his tears on K.'s jacket. K., upset, cleans the tears off his jacket.*)

WHIPPER: I can't wait any longer. (*Whips Franz, who hysterically throws himself towards K. screaming.*)

FRANZ: Mercy! Have mercy on me! (*Screams louder with each stroke. K. in anguish removes Franz from him with a certain violence.*)

K.: Enough! Enough! Don't you see that the staff may hear you. Enough! (*Closes the door. A knock on K.'s office door.*) It's me!

EMPLOYEE'S VOICE: Good evening, Sir. Has anything happened?

K.: No, no. There were just some dogs howling in the back yard. You may go back to your work. (*K., a bit to the public, a bit to himself.*) Bah! All those men are scoundrels. I saw his eyes glitter at the sight of the bills. I would have given them to him, since I really want to free the warders. And, above all, because I have started a fight against the corruption of justice. (*Goes back to the utility room door. Listens for a while. Nothing is*

38   *The Comic Trial of Joesph K.*

heard. Exits. The narrator enters. While he talks, he fixes the chair at K.'s desk.)

NARRATOR: Certainly Mr. K. couldn't be asked the sacrifice of intervening directly in this case. The truth was that he couldn't do anything else but abandon these men to the hands of the whipper and close the door leaving behind him a sepulchral silence. The next day, K. couldn't get the warders off his mind. (*Finishes fixing the chair. K. enters, pays him. The narrator thanks him and exits. K. goes nervously to the utility room. Everything is the same. The whipper is hitting the warders with his rod. Seeing K., they throw themselves towards him.*)

WARDERS: Sir! Sir! (*K. slams the door.*)

K.: (*Cries*) Kullisch! (*The employee enters, running.*) Clean this messy room, can't you? We're smothering in dirt! (*The employee nods. At the same time he gives K. a letter, which he does not read but tears up instead and slaps Kullisch. At that precise moment his Uncle Albert walks in. His posture is a little bent. Carries his Panama hat in his left hand and stretches out his right hand from the doorway. He would knock over everything in his way. The employee leaves surprised.*)

UNCLE ALBERT: My dear nephew! (*Greeting him.*) Excuse my hurry, but you know me. Always in a hurry, but, what do you expect? One has to get through one's business in the single day I spend in the city, and of course I can't let pass any business or meeting or (why not?) even a bit of entertainment. Well, giving myself some time, I have come to see you.

K.: I was sure you would come.

UNCLE: It was necessary for my peace of mind.

K.: Yes, sit down.

UNCLE: No, I'm sorry. I don't have the time. (*Intimately.*) I wish only to have a word with you. What is it I hear, Joseph? (*Takes several papers from K.'s desk and sits on them to keep his white suit from getting stained. Checks it.*) For God's sake, Joseph! Is it true? Can it be true?

K.: I can very well imagine what you're talking about. Without a doubt you've heard something about my trial.

UNCLE: Yes, that is so. My daughter Erna has written me about it. In fact, she tells me that you have come to calling me "the ghost from the past," a name that as a matter of fact I don't like. This very morning I received her letter. Here it is in my pocket. Would you care to read it?

K.: No, no. It's not necessary.

UNCLE: Oh! It's such a nice letter. I must confess to you that it made me cry.

K.: I don't doubt it.

UNCLE: I could read the passage about you.

K.: No, it's not necessary.

UNCLE: And, what do you say about all this?

K.: That it's all true. But don't worry. It isn't serious.

UNCLE: That's a nice thing to ask me! My dear Joseph, think of yourself, your parents, our good name. You have been, up until now, our pride, and you cannot turn into the disgrace of the family. Tell me; I'm sure it's something related to the bank.

K.: No, above all else, Uncle, this is no ordinary case.

UNCLE: But how did it happen? Why didn't you inform me? In a way I am still your tutor, and I'm proud of it. I'll do whatever I can to help you. The best thing for you to do would be to take a vacation and come with us to the country.

K.: Dear Uncle, trials are not won by nervousness. Don't worry. I willingly submit to your good sense. I just don't think your suggestion of my going to the countryside is advisable since it could be taken as a flight and therefore guilt. Nevertheless, we agree. What do you think is the first thing we should do?

UNCLE: We'll go to Lawyer Huld. We went to school together. You surely know him by name, don't you? You don't know him? How strange! He enjoys a great reputation as a defense attorney and lawyer for the poor. But beyond that he is a man of trust. Well, hurry! Hurry up! Hurry up! This is totally unheard of! Oh, good God, where are we going to end! (*They exit. The last words are heard from outside. Kullisch enters when they're gone.*)

KULLISCH: Well, that ass is gone! We will be finally able to go, too. (*Dark in the office space. A repeated knocking is heard. No one opens*).

UNCLE'S VOICE: Open the door! We're friends of Mr. Huld! (*A timid girl, pale, black eyes, and face of a doll; wears an apron and carries a candle; opens the door and runs to hide. Uncle and nephew walk in.*)

UNCLE: Next time be a little quicker to open the door. (*To K.*) Surely she is a new maid afraid of strangers. Let's go, Joseph. This maid will never invite us in. (*They walk through the interior.*)

LENI: Mr. Huld is ill.

UNCLE: Ill? You're saying . . . (*She nods.*) Is it his heart?

LENI: I believe so. (*Leads them to the lawyer's room. In another angle of the room which the candle doesn't illuminate just yet, a long bearded face lies on some pillows.*)

HULD: Who is it, Leni?

UNCLE: I'm Albert, your old friend.

HULD: Oh, Albert! (*Rises a little and falls back.*)

UNCLE: (*Sitting on the edge of the bed.*) How are you doing? I don't believe it. It is one of those heart attacks that will pass just like the others.

HULD: It's possible, but this is worse than the others. I can hardly breathe. I can't sleep.

UNCLE: Young girl, be so kind as to leave us alone for a while. I want to consult my friend on a personal matter.

LENI: (*Severely.*) You see that my master is ill, and he cannot be consulted.

UNCLE: You damned girl! . . . (*K. gets up and places his hand upon his uncle's mouth. The lawyer half rises. The uncle calms down.*) Please, go away.

HULD: (*Supplicant.*) In the presence of Leni, you may say anything you want.

UNCLE: This affair doesn't concern me. It's not a secret of mine but of my nephew, whom I have brought with me.

(*Introduces K.*) Mr. Joseph K., the sub-associate director of a bank.

HULD: Oh, pardon me, I had not seen that you were here! Go, Leni. (*She exits. Huld half rises a little.*) And about your nephew's case, it interests me. If my heart doesn't stay firm, at least it will have found a worthy obstacle to fail against.

UNCLE: (*To K.*) Did you hear, Joseph? What's the matter? Something bothering you?

K.: No, no. All of a sudden Mr. Huld reminded me of the Examining Magistrate who interrogated me during the first hearing of my trial.

HULD: Me? (*A noise as of breaking china comes from the hall.*)

K.: What was that noise? I'll go and see what happened. (*The light dims in the bedroom area. K. searches in the dark hall. He trips over a chest located underneath a judge's portrait. Leni takes him by the hand. K. is startled.*)

LENI: Nothing has happened. I just broke a plate against the wall to make you come. (*Pause.*) Come this way. I'll help you.

K.: It's a lofty room. No doubt the clients of the "lawyer to the poor" must feel quite uncomfortable before the grand desk. (*Leni sits next to him, presses him against the seat where he is sitting now. K. looks at the portrait. It's a man dressed in a toga, seated on a high golden throne that fills the entire painting. His attitude is not of pride, nor majestic, but of a violent gesture as if he were going to jump, perhaps to make a definitive observation or to pronounce a sentence.*)

K.: Perhaps that is my judge.

LENI: I know him. This portrait is when he was young, but it could be that he was never like that. In person he's quite small, almost a dwarf.

K.: Yet in spite of that, he seems to be seated on an impressive throne.

LENI: No! It's all scenography. He's really sitting on a kitchen chair with a box under him to make him look taller.

K.: Now that I have you so close I can feel that you emanate an exciting fragrance.

LENI: Like what?

K.: Bitter. Like pepper. (*Leni, excited, kisses him on the neck and hair.*) You are suffocating me. Ssshhhttt!

LENI: What?

K.: It's raining.

LENI: Yes. (*They kiss. K. reacts.*) What's happening?

K.: My uncle! He must be furious. (*Exits through the door towards the street. The noise of rain is heard. Dark. The light moves up to where Uncle Albert is standing under an umbrella. K. arrives guarding himself from the rain.*)

UNCLE: Joseph! How could you do it! You go and hide with that despicable, filthy whore, who to top it off is the lawyer's mistress, and you spend long hours with her and don't bother to come back. And here you leave me, your uncle, waiting for hours, in the rain. Feel me. I'm soaking wet from head to toe. Worried sick about you.

NARRATOR: The fact of the matter was that K. felt that his defense was not in good hands. So he thought it necessary to intervene directly. His first step was suggested by an industrialist, a client from the bank, who insinuated he should go see a painter named Titorelli, who was acquainted with many judges and who could advise him on how to be in close touch with influential people.

The curtain opens. The noise of hitting aluminum is heard. K. enters, looks down the escalator, goes up to the gallery throughout the hall and down through the spiral escalator.

NARRATOR: When he entered the building there was a baby crying next to the escalator, face down on the floor, his shrieks hardly heard because of the noise coming from the workshop at the other side of the corridor. At all this K. only cast a glance, concerned as he was with his own personal trial and to end his visit as soon as he possibly could. (*K. comes down the spiral escalator. K.'s office has been turned into a painter's work studio, Titorelli's. Inside, a little girl, slightly hunchbacked, puts lipstick on with a fine brush she takes from the painter's easel, which is covered with a shirt. There is in her attitude a premature lust.*)

K.: Does a painter named Titorelli live here? (*The girl runs to a corner next to K., laughing. She hits K. slightly with her elbow right on the stomach. K. reacts, disturbed. The girl nods her head.*)

GIRL: What do you want him for?

K.: Well, I'd like to know more about him. I want him to do a portrait of me.

GIRL: Your portrait? (*Hits him with her open hand, laughing boldly. A man dressed in a nightgown enters.*)

TITORELLI: Oh! (*He bows in profound reverence and holds out his hand to K.*) I'm the painter Titorelli. (*Invites K. to be seated. K. sits on the bed. From beneath the bed, all of a sudden a hand grabs him by the leg. K. screams frightened. Also from beneath the bed, another girl comes out, more or less of the same age, laughing stupidly. Titorelli runs after her and grabs her. He carries her out on his arms. The hunchbacked girl comes out at Titorelli's request, but tries to escape and get back in again. The painter prevents her. Through a broken pane of the door the faces of the two girls can be seen.*)

K.: You seem to be the sensation around here.

TITORELLI: (*Underneath the nightgown he's only wearing a yellow legged underpants, barefooted.*) Oh! Those brats! They are really annoying. (*Brings a chair and invites K. to sit down.*) One time I painted a portrait of one of them, and since then they've been after me. This really interferes with my work. If it weren't because I live in this studio for free I should have been gone long ago.

K.: Are you working on a painting?

TITORELLI: Yes, in a portrait, as a matter of fact. (*Removes the shirt from the canvas. It's the portrait of a judge.*)

K.: That must be a judge. And what about that figure on the back of the chair? Is that a sylph?

TITORELLI: No.

K.: Mercury?

TITORELLI: No.

K.: An archangel?

TITORELLI: No.

K.: What does it mean?
TITORELLI: Well, it still needs more detail. (*Takes a brush and retouches.*) It is . . . justice.

K.: Ah! Now I recognize it. There's the blindfold over the eyes, and here is the scale. But, aren't those wings on the figure's heels? Is it going to fly?

TITORELLI: Yes, those are wings. I have instructions to paint it like that. Actually, it is justice and the goddess of victory represented in one single image.

K.: (*Laughing.*) Well, they don't make a very good combination, though. Justice should not move at all, or else the scales would move, and then it would be impossible to dictate a just verdict.

TITORELLI: (*The joke isn't funny for him.*) I followed my client's instructions.

K.: Yes, yes, of course. Well, more than justice or the goddess of victory, it seems more like Diana, the goddess of the hunt. (*Titorelli turns to K., annoyed.*)

TITORELLI: Why don't you take off your coat? It's hot in here, isn't it?

K.: I feel more like a heavy atmosphere. (*K. sits on the edge of the bed, takes off his coat, and considering how hot it is, he takes off his jacket too, loosening his tie.*)

VOICES OF THE GIRLS: (*Morbid screams and laughter.*) He took off his jacket! He took off his jacket!

TITORELLI: The girls think that I'm going to paint your portrait because you took off your jacket.

K.: Ah!

TITORELLI: And tell me one thing, Mr. K. Are you innocent?

K.: (*Surprised by the question. Hesitates.*) Yes, yes. Absolutely. (*In spite of his comments, he doesn't seem to be at all convinced of his innocence.*) It is the first time that anyone has asked me face to face.

TITORELLI: Well, if you're innocent, the problem is very simple. But . . . are you innocent?

K.: Of course I am!

VOICE OF GIRL 1: Titorelli, is that man leaving soon?

VOICE OF GIRL 2: Are you going to paint his portrait? (*K. is embarrassed, doesn't know what to do.*)

VOICE OF GIRL 1: Don't paint him, please. He's very ugly!

TITORELLI: (*Gets up and opens the door. The girls try to come in.*) Shut up! If you don't stop making all that noise I'll throw you down the stairs. (*They obey at once.*) Excuse me. (*Whispers into K.'s ear.*) These girls belong to the court.

K.: What?

TITORELLI: As you heard it. Well, I'll find a way to get you out of all this. Here the only thing that matters is the pull one may have. Personal contacts with high officials. Ah! I almost forgot to ask you what kind of acquittal you would prefer. There are three possibilities: definite acquittal is without a doubt the best. Now that I recall, I have never known a case of definite acquittal. We only know of legendary cases. They're so beautiful. I myself have painted several pictures inspired by those stories.

K.: And what are the other two possibilities?

TITORELLI: One is the affidavit of your innocence. In this case I go to all the judges I know to have them subscribe to the affidavit. The judges in charge of your case, taking in consideration that the affidavit is signed by other judges, will acquit you without any doubt. Then you walk out of the court in absolute freedom.

K.: In absolute freedom?

TITORELLI: Well, only ostensibly, because it happens that one day, another judge may notice that the accusation is still valid, order the arrest of the accused, and so the case is opened one more time. (*To K., who is in total despair.*) C'mon, man! Don't be downcast. Perhaps you would prefer indefinite postponement. This is nothing more than your recognition of your status of an accused man, presented systematically before the judge. (*K. rises.*)

VOICES OF THE GIRLS: He got up! He got up!

TITORELLI: Are you leaving?

K.: No, I've developed a headache with all those explanations.

TITORELLI: In reality it's very simple. Both methods prevent the accused from being sentenced.

K.: Yes, but they also prevent the final acquittal.

TITORELLI: Exactly! You've got it!

K.: I'll come back soon. (*Throws his coat over his shoulders and walks towards the door. Tries to go out. The girls, laughing, stop him.*)

TITORELLI: Wait a minute. Wouldn't you like to see one or two of my paintings that I could sell to you? (*Goes underneath the bed. Pulls out a stack of stretched canvases. Titorelli blows, and the dust blinds K., makes him cough. Referring to the painting.*) "Wild Nature". (*Shows it to him.*) Two threes in the middle of the dark grass. And, as a background, a sunset full of different shades of color.

K.: (*Trying to be polite.*) Yeah, it's nice. I'll buy it.

TITORELLI: (*Pulls out another canvas.*) Look, this is the matching one.

K.: No kidding. They're identical. Anyway, it doesn't matter. I'll buy both.

TITORELLI: I'm glad that you like my paintings. I'll give you all of my works. They're all sunsets. I've painted them by the dozens. Fortunately there are always sensitive people like yourself who like these paintings full of melancholy. (*Opens the door next to the bed, and K. is about to exit.*)

K.: But, what's this? Are these the court offices? I didn't know they were here.

TITORELLI: Why do you act so surprised? Everything is part of the court. (*The door is open, and all of a sudden the two girls come in and grab K. They're supposed to have come around the studio. The painter laughs.*) Until our next meeting, and don't take too long to decide! (*K. exits, running away from the girls. Blackout.*)

NARRATOR: K. considered that the lawyer Huld wasn't doing much pertaining to his trial, so he decided to dismiss him from his case.

The bell rings in Huld's house. A small man in shirt-sleeves, with a long beard, carrying a candle in one hand, goes to the door and peers through the eye hole. Leni dressed in a shirt appears in the hall.

BLOCK: It's him! (*The bell rings again. The little man opens. K. enters. Leni hides abruptly.*)

K.: (*Almost pushes Block with the door.*) Couldn't you be a little faster? (*Looks at him.*) Are you employed here?

BLOCK: (*Nervous, shy.*) No, I don't belong to the house. I'm just a client. I've come here on court business.

K.: In your shirt-sleeves?

BLOCK: (*Embarrassed.*) Oh! Excuse me!

K.: Is Leni your lover?

BLOCK: (*Horrified.*) Oh, God! No, no. Why do you think so?

K.: (*Smiles. Notices his own lack of trust.*) Hmm, you seem to be a decent man. What is your name?

BLOCK: Block. I'm a tradesman. (*Tries to turn back to hold out his hand to K. to introduce himself. K. pushes him without letting him stop.*)

K.: Is that your real name?

BLOCK: Of course. Why do you doubt it?

K.: I thought you might have a reason to conceal your name. (*Block attempts to leave. K. stops him by the suspenders.*) Why so fast? Bring the light over here. (*Searches the corners looking for Leni. Pushes Block away and treats him rudely.*) Do you know where Leni is hiding?

BLOCK: Hiding? No, she must be preparing soup for the lawyer.

K.: Why didn't you tell me so from the very beginning?

BLOCK: I was going to tell you, but you took me over there.

K.: You think you're very smart, don't you? Take me into the kitchen. (*Leni enters with a bowl of soup.*)

LENI: Good evening, Joseph.

K.: Good evening. (*K. waves the tradesman to sit down. The man obeys. To Leni.*) Who is this man?

LENI: (*takes K. by the waist.*) Just a miserable man. A tradesman named Block.

K.: Is he your lover? (*Leni tries to kiss him. K. fends her off.*)

LENI: But, Joseph! You wouldn't be jealous of Mr. Block, would you? (*To Block.*) Rudi, leave the candle alone. Come and help me. This gentleman suspects me.

BLOCK: (*Precipitately.*) I can't see in my mind you being jealous of us two.

K.: No, neither can I. (*K. and Leni laugh at the man.*)

LENI: (*Intimately.*) Forget about him. You can see now what kind of man he is. I have given him some considerations because he's one of the best clients. And? Do you want to see the lawyer? He's not doing very well, but if you want I'll tell him you're here, under the condition that you spend the night with me. (*K. takes off his coat and his hat, hangs them up.*)

BLOCK: (*Softly.*) Are you one of the lawyer's clients?

K.: That's none of your business!

LENI: You shut up! (*To K.*) I'm going to take him the soup now.

K.: Leni, I'm thinking I'm going to dismiss the lawyer. (*Leni turns back.*)

LENI: What?

K.: (*Surprised. Pause. Thinks.*) Nothing, hurry up! (*Leni exits. K. talks to Block.*) You're an old client of the lawyer's, aren't you?

BLOCK: Yes, an old client.

K.: How long has he been in charge of your affairs?

BLOCK: Well, of my grain business, more than twenty years, and of my trial — and that is probably what you're asking about — it's been more than five years now. (*Consults his little note pad.*) If you like, I can give you the exact dates. (*K. pulls up a chair next to Block.*)

K.: So, the lawyer also has an ordinary practice?

BLOCK: Of course. They even say that he his better at ordinary practice than any other practice.

K.: Hmm! That makes me feel better.

BLOCK: (*Puts his hand to his lips.*) What did I just say? Please, don't give me away! I beg you!

K.: Don't worry. I am no gossip.

BLOCK: The lawyer is too vindictive. And when he gets mad he makes no distinction. Perhaps I shouldn't be telling you this. but . . . I am really being unfaithful to him.

K.: What? Tell me; tell me.

BLOCK: Well, I'll tell you, but just in part. Then you'll have to tell me one of your secrets, so this way both of us will have something to hide.

K.: Fine, I'll tell you a secret so you can be calm. So now tell me. How is it that you're not faithful to the lawyer?

BLOCK: (*Doubtfully.*) Well, I have five more lawyers besides Doctor Huld.

K.: And why so many?

BLOCK: I don't want to lose my case. So if anything comes along that might offer the slightest hope, I wouldn't dare to reject it. This is the reason I've spent up to the last penny I had from my business.

K.: So you work on your own defense? I'd like you to tell me about that.

BLOCK: There isn't much to tell. It's an exhausting job, and the results are disappointing. To wait up in the corridor, just to keep your own trial in sight, to sit about and wait for your turn. I was in the corridor when you passed through.

K.: Oh, yes. When everybody stood up. I suppose they took me for a judge.

BLOCK: No, we stood up because the usher was coming with you. We knew you were just an accused man.

K.: The other day, when I went into the offices of the court, did the accused men make any comments?

BLOCK: Nonsense.

K.: What nonsense?

BLOCK: Things without any logic. People take refuge in superstition. One of them is based on the idea that from the accused's face and particularly from the line of his lips you can tell which will be the final result of your trial.

K.: (*Touching his lips.*) And what will be the result of mine?

BLOCK: That you'll be found guilty, and that your sentence won't take long.

K.: (*Pause.*) My lips? (*Draws out a small mirror and examines himself. Gesticulates.*) I don't see anything special about my lips. Do you?

LENI: Aha! How close together you are! (*K. and Block realize this and pull back to a more appropriate distance.*)

K.: Did you announce me?

LENI: The lawyer is waiting for you. Now leave Block alone. He has to go to sleep.

K.: He sleeps here?

LENI: Not everyone is like you, Joseph: getting to be seen by the lawyer at anytime you choose. Doesn't it surprise you that a sick man would receive you at eleven o'clock at night?

K.: He receives me because I'm his client.

BLOCK: The lawyer has other reasons to receive this gentleman. His case is of more interest than mine. It's only in its beginnings and probably in a hopeful stage. You'll see a difference later on.

LENI: Blabber-mouth! You mustn't believe a word he says. He talks too much. That's why the lawyer can't stand him. One time he took three days to receive him, and if Block isn't there when he calls him, he loses his opportunity, and again he has to make an appointment to be received. So he has to be ready. Day and night.

BLOCK: Yes, and as time goes by, one slowly becomes the lawyer's subordinate. (*K. walks towards the bedroom. Block stops him.*) Mr. Sub-Associate Director! (*K. stops.*) You have forgotten your promise. You were going to tell me one of your secrets.

K.: True. Well, although it's already an open secret, this very moment I'm going to dismiss the lawyer from my case.

BLOCK: Dismiss him! (*Runs through the room yelling with his arms up high.*) He is going to dismiss his lawyer! (*Leni tries to stop K., pushing Block aside, who gets in the way. K. enters the lawyer's room and tries to lock the door. Leni doesn't allow him. Finally K. locks the door.*)

HULD: (*Reading a document with his glasses on.*) I've been waiting for you a long time. I won't see you this late again. Sit down.

K.: (*Pulls up a chair.*) If you allow me.

HULD: I thought I heard you locking the door.

K.: Yes, I did it because of Leni.

HULD: Was she inopportune again?

K.: Inopportune?

HULD: Yes... (*Laughs, until he starts to cough and almost chokes. Laughs again.*) I suppose you have noticed that she's become inopportune towards you. (*Pats K.*) It's a peculiarity of hers. She finds almost all the accused men beautiful. (*Silence. Pause.*) She becomes attached to all of them. (*K. reacts.*) She loves them all, and it's evident that she is loved in return. It doesn't surprise me, as much as it seems to surprise you.

K.: Dr. Huld, you invariably attempt to distract the attention from the essential matter by just speaking of other things. The essential is, what has been achieved in my defense?

HULD: Hmm! I see your attitude today is more hostile than usual. Are you coming here to see me for any particular reason?

K.: Yes, I've come to tell you that as of today you're dismissed from my trial.

HULD: (*Pause.*) Did I understand well?

K.: I hope so.

HULD: Well, it's a plan we can discuss.

K.: It's not a plan. It's a fact.

HULD: Maybe, but we shouldn't rush too much.

K.: I beg you not to use the word "we." You give me the impression that you wish not to accept my decision not to represent me any longer, as if you were trying to continue as my advisor. What I've just told you, is not a hurried decision. (*He rises.*) I've thought about it extensively, perhaps too extensively. My decision is final.

HULD: Well, allow me to make a few comments. (*He wears a blanket at all times as if it were chilly. He sits on the edge of the bed. His bare legs are exposed.*)

K.: Well, it's not necessary to expose yourself to catching a cold.

HULD: I have my reasons. Your uncle is a friend of mine, and as time goes by I've become fond of you, too, and it's nothing to be ashamed of. (*Pause.*)

K.: I appreciate your gesture, but for some time now I've been thinking that your efforts are not enough.

HULD: I understand; I understand. You're feeling impatient.

K.: (*A little irritated.*) It's not a matter of impatience.

HULD: (*Laughing kindly.*) After all this time in one's practice, nothing really new comes along. How many clients have stood before me, speaking to me in the same terms you're using now! I can assure you that there are poor creatures ready to fling themselves at any crumb I throw. Some of us lawyers carry our clients on our shoulders, restlessly. And even so, I don't regret devoting myself to this hard task. Although as is happening with you, my work is totally misunderstood.

K.: I warn you, your speech, instead of convincing me, is making me impatient. So I have to get through with this at once. (*Pause.*) What steps are you planning to take in case I keep you on as my representative?

58   The Comic Trial of Joesph K.

HULD: I'll continue with the procedures already underway.

K.: Ha! Then it's of no use to keep on with this conversation.

HULD: (*Victorious.*) I'll make a new attempt. I have the impression that your bad opinion about the way I have conducted myself is because of the soft way you have been treated in spite of your status of an accused man. At times it's better to be in chains than to be free. I would like to show you the way I treat other accused men. You might learn something. Open the door and sit down here.

K.: Alright, which doesn't imply that you may change my decision. (*Huld lies down with the blanket over his knees. Turns his back to the public. Rings the bell. K. opens the door. Leni eavesdropping. She enters and casts a quick glance trying to figure out what's going on. She smiles at K., who doesn't respond.*)

HULD: Bring Block!

LENI: (*Yells out.*) Block, the lawyer needs you! (*Leni goes to K. She notices the lawyer is facing the wall, and she strokes K.'s hair. They tussle briefly. K. ends up controlling her. Block comes in quickly. He is undecided whether to step into the room and stays in the doorway. No one tells him to come in. He doesn't know what to do. Finally he enters on his tip toes with an expression of anxiety, clutching his hands.*)

HULD: Are you there, Block?

BLOCK: (*Terrified, he stumbles. The question strikes Block as if he had been hit on the chest and back with a stick. He recovers himself and bows.*) At your service.

HULD: What do you want? You have come at the wrong time.

BLOCK: (*Disturbed, getting ready to leave.*) But wasn't I called?

HULD: You have been called, and yet you have come at the wrong time.

BLOCK: (*Like a child being punished, he looks into a distant corner, without moving.*) Do you want me to go?

HULD: Well, since you're here, stay! (*Block trembles.*) Yesterday I saw my friend, the third judge, and we spoke about your case. Do you want to know what he said?

BLOCK: Yes, yes, please. (*The lawyer doesn't answer. Block flings himself to his knees by the bed. K.rises.*)

K.: (*Upset, lifts Block.*) What are you doing? (*Leni tries to stop him. He repels her. She complains.*)

HULD: (*Raising his voice, furious.*) Who is your lawyer?

BLOCK: You are.

HULD: Who else besides me?

BLOCK: No one; no one but you.

HULD: Then, don't pay any attention to anyone but me!

BLOCK: (*To K.*) You see? Stay out of it!

K.: (*Surprised.*) Go ahead. Kneel. Crawl on all fours if you want. I don't give a damn!

BLOCK: (*Throws himself against K., hitting him on the chest with his fists.*) You're not to talk to me like that. I won't allow it. And certainly not in the presence of the lawyer, who admits us

60   *The Comic Trial of Joesph K.*

here only out of charity. You're an accused man like me. And I'm a gentleman just like you, if not better.

K.: (*Surprised.*) Don't you see? The lawyer is humiliating you deliberately to intimidate me and get me to acquiesce, too.

BLOCK: (*Runs to the lawyer's bed, accusing K.*) Doctor Huld, did you hear what this man said to me? He is a newcomer. My trial has lasted five years, and he dares to advise me. He even insults me. I, who have studied all rules of obedience, devotion, and self-giving.

HULD: Don't pay any attention. Do what you think is best.

BLOCK: Thank you. (*He kneels next to the bed.*) I'm on my knees, Doctor Huld. (*Caressing the quilt.*)

LENI: (*Lets go of K., who had seized her by the hand.*) You're hurting me! Let go of me! I want to be with Block. (*Goes towards the tradesman and sits on the edge of the bed. Block, mimicking, implores Leni to intervene with the lawyer in his favor. Leni points at the lawyer's hand, to kiss it. Block does so. The lawyer remains silent. Leni lies down close to the lawyer and strokes his hair. In a sweet voice.*) Tell him.

HULD: I don't know if I should tell him.

LENI: Why do you hesitate?

HULD: How has he behaved today? (*Block takes Leni's hand and looks at her imploringly.*)

LENI: He's been quiet and hard-working.

HULD: You're praising him, and you do nothing but to make what I have to say more difficult.

LENI: Wasn't the judge's opinion favorable?

HULD: No, it wasn't favorable. He even told me, "Don't talk to me about that man, Block." "But he is a client of mine," I replied. "I don't believe that his case is lost. It's true that he is personally repulsive, has bad manners, is dirty. But as a client he is beyond reproach." And he answered, "What do you think he would say if he knew that his trial hasn't even begun yet? That the bell hasn't been rung to start the sessions?" (*Block tries to get up.*) Quiet there, Block! (*Block stops, his knees trembling, and he finally falls down.*) Don't panic at every word you hear! If you become afraid once more, I will never inform you of anything again. Have you no confidence in me? What's wrong with you? You're still alive and under my protection. Your panic upsets me. It reflects your lack of confidence in me! (*Block listens while pulling lint from the carpet.*)

LENI: Block! (*Jerking him by the neck.*) Stop pulling the carpet hair and listen to the lawyer. (*Block gets up and slowly leaves the scene. Long silence.*)

HULD: Well, Mr. K., were you saying? What did you say your decision was?

K.: Well. (*Rises, walks towards the exit.*) I . . . don't know. Perhaps it would be best if I think about it more carefully. (*Exits the room. The lawyer looks at Leni with a smile on his face. Dark. K.'s office is lighted.*)

NARRATOR: What a stupor overcame K. at the idea of taking on his own defense! What would happen? What kind of life awaited him? Now that he was at the apogee of his professional career and on the verge of becoming the rival of the vice president. (*K. rushes into his office, followed by Kullisch. Carries a coat, scarf, hat, his hand on his forehead.*)

K.: (*Glances through the door to see some clients.*) Ah! Why did they have to come at such an inappropriate time? I'm not in for anyone! (*Kullisch about to exit.*) Kullisch! (*The man returns, scared.*) Tell those gentlemen waiting for me in the waiting room that I cannot see them today, if they would be so kind to return tomorrow. Take all calls and do not allow anyone into my office. I'm quite busy at a very important task, and also, I have a headache and a terrible cold. (*The employee exits, closing the door.*) Now that the nights have become too short to enjoy the pleasures of a bachelor's life, now I have to take care of my own trial, and while this trial develops I have to dedicate my attention to the bank's affairs. Is the bank ever going to take this into consideration when evaluating my work performance? Never! Neither for me, nor for anyone! (*Sniffs. During the whole scene he's got a book in his hand. Opens the book and reads.*) "Io sono malato. Von avere voglia di parlare. Avere altro cose da fare. Avore molto lavoro. Debo mostrare la catedrale. Finisco, finiamo, finíte, finíscamo." (*Throws the book on top of the desk. Drops face down. Sleeps and dreams. Enter Miss Bürstner dressed as a bullfighter. She walks down the office. K calls her. She exits. The phone rings. K., furious, goes to answer.*) Didn't I say ... yes, yes. Ah! it's you, Leni. Bad, yes, very bad. My birthday? Ah! yes, it's true. Yes, I'm 31 years old; yes, yes, yes. I appreciate it, but I have a horrible headache. Yes, a cold. Excuse me, but I don't have time to talk to you. I have to go to the cathedral. I have been asked to show some artistic treasures to an Italian colleague. Yes, he is one of the bank's clients. The appointment is at ten in the morning, and it's already past nine thirty. Ciao. (*The woman keeps on talking.*) Yes. Ciao. Yes, I speak a really bad Italian; yesterday when I was speaking to this man in the director's office I didn't understand a word. Nothing. And, besides, he's got a long perfumed mustache. And as hard as I try, I am unable to read his lips. I have tried to comunicate with him in French. He speaks it so badly that we can't understand each other. I'm desperate. I didn't sleep. I spent all night going over my

Italian grammar! (*Furious, he hangs up. Doesn't notice that the assistant manager has entered the room. He looks around, notices the book of Italian grammar, and begins reading it. K. sees him. Grabs the book. Slaps his hand. Puts the book in his pocket. Puts on his hat and scarf. Opens the door and exits.*)

ASSISTANT MANAGER: Mr. K., there are two men sitting in the waiting room. They are waiting for you to receive them. Listen, Mr. K., are you leaving? And what about these gentlemen? I think they have been waiting a long time for you.

K.: We have had an arrangement.

ASSISTANT MANAGER: (*To the clients.*) Mr. K., I suppose these gentlemen wouldn't stay waiting for hours if their affairs weren't of the utmost importance, not to say urgent. Well, Mr. K., there is a simple solution: I'll put myself at the disposal of these gentlemen to help them, in your place. Naturally, your problems should be treated immediately. We are businessmen, and we know what time is worth for all of us.

K.: (*Apart. To the assistant manager*) How clever you are to invade the territory I have to abandon!

ASSISTANT MANAGER: Gentlemen. Would you be so kind as to come into my office? (*He invites them into K.'s office. K. leaves, furious.*)

(*The light dims slowly. A spotlight illuminates the narrator in a corner of the stage as he speaks. The curtain closes to prepare for the cathedral, or the scene can be prepared as he speaks. In the distance a bell tolls.*)

NARRATOR: The main square was deserted. K. had been punctual. It was exactly ten o'clock when he entered the cathedral. The Italian man had not arrived yet. In the rain, K. walked around the building to make sure that the Italian wasn't waiting for him in a side door. He did not see him anywhere, so, tired and soaking wet, he reentered the cathedral.

The curtain opens, or someone lights three long wax candles. K. enters. The picture of the judge in the lawyer's house has been substituted for a religious image. K. enters through a big, hand-carved door like that of a chapel, walking slowly and looking with respect and solemnity at everything in his path. Stops before the picture and examines it carefully. The picture can't be seen with clarity, and K. draws up a small lamp, lighting the picture. Next to the picture, a woman prays, while the narrator awaits leaning against a column. K. looks at him a bit surprised and waves pleasantly. The priest, at the foot of the spiral stair, waves at K., making signals he does not understand.

K.: (*To the narrator.*) Pardon me. Have you seen an Italian man around here?

NARRATOR: Excuse me?

K.: An Italian . . . No. (*Pause.*) I never noticed that pulpit before. (*The priest waves at him.*) What does that man want? Do I look like a suspect? Is he after a tip? (*The priest sniffs.*) What does he have in his left hand?

NARRATOR: Rappee.

K.: Ah! Yeah. What would he want?

NARRATOR: For you to kneel and bless. (*K. does so.*)

K.: But is he going to preach a sermon? To an empty church? (*The priest walks up the stairs. To the narrator.*) If I don't leave now I won't be able to until it ends. (*The narrator exits.*)

PRIEST: (*In a well cultivated voice that echoes through the church.*) Joseph K.! (*K. stops. Looking down at the floor. After a brief pause he turns slowly to the priest up in the pulpit, who waves him nearer.*)

K.: Me? (*K. comes back and takes a seat. The priest nods, indicating a seat closer to the pulpit. K. obeys, goes and sits down. The proximity of the pulpit makes him pull his head back and look up to see the priest.*)

PRIEST: You are Joseph K. You are an accused man.

K.: Yes, so I've been told.

PRIEST: Then you are the man I'm looking for. I'm the prison chaplain. I made you come to have a conversation with you.

K.: Oh! I didn't know! I just came to show the cathedral to an Italian man.

PRIEST: Are you aware that your trial is going badly?

K.: Yes, but I'm going to seek more help.

PRIEST: (*Recriminating and upset.*) You trust too much to the help of others and especially from women.

K.: Well, sometimes women have a great influence. If I could only convince some of them . . . (*He laughs a little. The attitude of the priest freezes his smile. Pause.*) Sorry, I didn't mean to offend you.

PRIEST: (*Yelling.*) Don't you have eyes to see?

K.: (*Upset.*) Why don't you come down from there? If you come down from the pulpit, maybe you could give me valuable advice, even if you are a part of justice.

PRIEST: (*Yelling.*) The court is sacred . . . (*Pause. Silence.*) Excuse me. I'll come down now. (*Takes a lamp and carries it with him.*) I first had to talk to you from above. Otherwise I'd have let myself be easily influenced. (*K. helps him.*)

K.: You are very good to me. You are different from anyone else who belongs to the court. I have more trust in you, even though I don't know you very well.

PRIEST: Don't be deluded about the court. This delusion is described in the writings as: "Before the law stands a doorkeeper. (*Pause.*) One day a man from the country comes and begs the doorkeeper to let him in. But the doorkeeper replies that he cannot admit him. The man on reflection asks if he will be allowed later. "Perhaps," answers the doorkeeper, "but not now." Since the door that gives access to the law stands open, as usual, and the doorkeeper steps to one side, the man bends to peer through the door. When the doorkeeper sees him, he laughs and says, "If you are so desirous, try to get in without my permission. But note that I am powerful." And when he sees more closely the doorkeeper in his fur robe, his big pointed nose, and his long tarter beard (*describing himself*) he decides that it would be better for him to wait until he gets permission to enter. (*The priest seems like a sorcerer telling a horror story to a child. K. looks at him, absorbed. He brings the light onto the priest, and the similarity between the priest and tale is evident: K. is the country man, and the priest is the guardian of the law. The scene develops at the church door. The priest seems not to allow K. to exit, who seems to want to try, but doesn't dare. The priest takes a chair and sits K. at the side of the door.*) Then the doorkeeper gives him a stool for him to sit down on by the door. And he has been sitting there for many years. He makes many attempts to get in, and he annoys the doorkeeper with his persistence. The guardian impersonally ends up telling him that he isn't allowed to enter yet. (*In guardian's voice.*) "Yes, and when the man grows old and mutters, his eyes grow dim, and he no longer can tell if night has fallen or his eyes are failing him. His life is coming to an end. Before he dies, all he has experienced is reduced in his mind to a question he had never before asked of the doorkeeper..."

K.: (*Completing the idea.*) If the whole world is interested in the law, how can it be possible that in all these years I have been the only one who has come to you to be admitted?

PRIEST: (*Nods to K., indicating that that is the precise question.*) Exactly. The guardian, who understands that the man is close to his end and that he can barely hear, bends down and yells into his ear: "No one else but you could have been admitted, since that door was intended for you alone. Now I am going to leave and shut it." (*The priest closes the door through which a stream of light enters.*)

K.: (*Very interested.*) So the usher deceived that man.

PRIEST: To doubt him would be to doubt the law.

K.: Sad opinion that turns a lie into a universal principle. And, also, it's such a confusing story that I only want to put it out of my mind. (*They are walking away from the door. The light from the lamp dims down.*) I shall go now. I'm the sub-associate director of a bank, and they're waiting for me. You see, I just came here to show the cathedral to a foreign client.

PRIEST: Well, then go. (*Takes the lamp.*)

K.: But, I can't find my way out in this darkness.

PRIEST: Turn left till you find the wall. Then keep on going, and you'll come to the door. (*The priest puts out the light and leaves.*)

K.: (*Scared.*) Wait a minute. My urgency to get back to the bank is nothing, really. I can stay longer. (*Begins to walk in the darkness, and he comes across two pale men dressed in tuxedoes and high hats.*) Do you want something from me? (*The men nod kindly, and they point to each other.*) They send me two low-class actors. They want to finish me off with almost no effort. In what theater do you act? Are you tenors? I mean because of your double chins. (*Yelling.*) Of all people, why did they have to send you?! (*A woman enters and walks up the stairs and down the hall. She seems to be Miss Bürstner.*) Miss Bürstner! (*To one of the executioners.*) Well, I'm not sure. If it's she, it's of no importance. The only thing I can do now is to keep my serenity and my analytical ability until the end. All my life I wanted to embrace too much and not always for a laudable motive. It's been a mistake. And now I'm to show that less than one whole year of trial hasn't taught me anything? Should I leave this world as an insect? Wouldn't people say, after my departure, that at the beginning of my trial I wanted to finish it, and at the end I wanted to start it over again? No, I don't want that to be said. I congratulate myself for having been sent these two half deaf and dumb creatures for companionship, and that they have given me the opportunity to tell myself what must be done.

EXECUTIONERS: (*The executioners take off their hats and bow, each offering the other the priority of starting their duty.*) Be so kind, please. After you. No, no way. You first, etc. (*Finally one of them goes to K. and takes off his jacket, his vest, and the shirt. K. trembles unwillingly, and the executioner gives him a pat on the back to comfort him and folds K.'s clothes, placing them neatly in a pile. The other one, who has found a certain spot, calls his companion. They both throw K. to the floor. He is uncomfortable. They try to arrange him, but they can't. Finally one of them opens his tuxedo and draws out a long, double-edged butcher knife. He examines the sharp edges. The courtesies are repeated. They pass the knife to each other in front of K.'s face, inviting each other to proceed.*)

K.: If you're thinking that I'm going to take that knife and plunge it into me chest, you're wrong. First of all, I don't have the necessary strength, and second it's your duty as officials, and I am not about to relieve you of your responsibility. (*Right then a human figure glances from above and releases a cry of pain, then retires. K. turns to her.*)

K.: Who was that? A friend? Someone who sympathized? Or was it just a person? Was it mankind? Is there hope still? Are there arguments in my favor that have been overlooked? Of course there must be. It's true that logic is doubtless, but it cannot resist a man who wants to go on living. Where is the judge whom I have never seen? Where is the high court, to which I have never penetrated? (*The hand of one of the executioners grabs K.'s neck. K. lifts his hands, spreading his fingers. The other one plunges the knife in K.'s heart, then repeats it twice. Both men watch his agony closely. K. with failing eyes looks at his executioners and turns to the public. He seems to says something and falls dead. The cry of a child is heard. The assassins clean the knife in a tragic-comic pantomime routine and exit.*)

NARRATOR: "Like a dog!" said K., before he died, and it was as if the shame of it should outlive him. (*Music. The actor interpreting the role of K. gets up.*)

ACTOR: Franz died in June of 1924. His life-long obsession was the search for strength and hope. (*Draws a book from his pocket. The cover reads "DIARY." He reads:* "Literature is not much a matter of literary history but a people's matter." *Closes the book. The actor moves the priest aside from the door. The priest seems to be offended by this, but he moves stiffly. K. stops him by the shoulders, takes the door handle to open the door to exit, but he stops instead. To the public.*) "Strong rain," said Franz. "Face the rain. Let its fierce beating soak you. Slip through the water that means to drag you down. But in spite of everything, resist." (*Opens the door. A warm stream of light enters.*) Wait standing for the sun that enters suddenly and endlessly in

70   *The Comic Trial of Joesph K.*

torrents. (*Music. The actor exits or enters through the door towards the light. They all exit through that door. The light dims down to a blackout, or the curtain closes.*)

THE END

Figure 6. "I bet this is something organized by my colleagues at the bank because today is my birthday."

Prologue

Augusto Monterroso

    Five in the evening. Hector Ortega arrives. He brings a copy of his stage adaptation of Kafka's *The Trial*, which he means to revise and publish as a book, "lightening some dialogues." Of course, we talk for more than two hours on the subject of Kafka in his condition of humorist and what seems to be a recurrent topic in this house: whether it's correct to comply with the writer's last wish. After all, Kafka did ask his most intimate friend to burn his writings after his death.

    Ortega shows me photographs by Cuellar of the stage presentation of his adaptation and copies of the drawings and pictures of the scenography by José Luis Cuevas. "They would fit the book nicely," he tells me with enthusiasm and admiration for Cuevas's work, and I agree. We recall Orson Welles's adaptations for the cinema and André Gide/Jean Louis Barrault's for the theater. Gide and Barrault worked with Kafka's transcendentalism and metaphysics (and why shouldn't they if that's how they saw it?), to which Kafka had turned thirty or forty years ago. Finally, I shyly read him portions of a page of a book of mine from 1972 where I pointed out Kafka's humor and recalled Max Brod's witness to the delight with which his friend, not yet ready to have his writings burned, read chapters of *The Trial* to him.

Figure 7. "Beatle." Augusto Monterroso.

Notes on the Stage Adaptation of Franz Kafka's *The Trial*

Héctor Ortega

Kafka is a writer so vast that he can be appreciated from an infinity of angles. In this stage adaptation of *The Trial* I intended to stress only one of them. Perhaps I've exaggerated in taking a side (Gogol says that a speech cannot be launched without exaggerating a little), but I'm sure I have exaggerated much less than Jean Louis Barrault and André Gide did, or even Orson Welles himself accentuating the tragic and pathetic side of the novel and eliminating any humorous dash that could compromise his gloomy conception and inspire a laugh. There is no doubt in my mind that through their famous stage adaptation Barrault and Gide were influential, in their time, notably in Europe but also throughout the rest of the world, giving Kafka's work the intimate and metaphysical character to which it has been reduced for so long.

The Traditional Conception of the Kafkaesque Character

Before anything else one must make several pertinent clarifications: Joseph K. is not a lesser employee wearing threadbare, gray clothes as is generally believed. On the contrary, K. is a successful, lordly, elegant bureaucrat who carries a cane and spends his weekends at a prestigious club communing with respectable bankers, and afterwards, past midnight, he happens to visit a young lover. His income allows him to live comfortably in a boarding house and still have money left over to carry around in his pocket. The wardens who announce to him that a prosecution case against him has been opened state that apparently he spends a great part of his pay on fine imported suits and shirts, not to mention silk pajamas.

For better or worse, and although it's not at all defined, K. is a man in a position close to the "second-ranked man in the financial institution" in which he works. One might say that he is somewhat the "sub-associate director" of an important bank, even if this is an appointed position, so the notion that K. is poor is another of the false myths that revolve around Kafka's novel and that have greatly influenced interpretations of both the character and the general context in which he evolves.

If we were to make an ethical judgment of Joseph K.'s character, he could be defined as a competitive, misogynous, inconsistent, arrogant, proud, and insolent opportunist, a scorner. (We need only be reminded of the way he refers to his employees at large when the inspector arrives at his room; Joseph K. takes offense because the man calls his subalterns "his colleagues." "They are employees of a lesser category," he states. On another occasion, referring to one of them he says, "I detest him as I do the others. He'll never ascend in spite of his repulsive, humble humility.")

One might make an interesting and humorous observation about the author of "Report to the Academy" (in which the narrator is an ape), or "Investigations of a Dog" (in which the main character is a speaking dog), or the short story that tells of those horrible little balls jumping onto the protagonist's back, "The Metamorphosis," in which Gregor Samsa becomes a hideous bug. These stories are famous for their expressionism, though in the specific case of *The Trial*, we are dealing with a naturalist novel. Here there are no extraordinary events. The places and events described are all possible or real (except for some small details, such as when Joseph K. casually arrives at his trial on a Sunday and he has been expected, a really strange thing, or when the janitor's room at his office turns into a place where the agents are whipped after having been denounced, or the whipper's leather outfit, but even this could be possible). Perhaps the only clearly symbolic event is that, just as in *The Castle*—although here the novel's title itself warns us—all the spaces of the social structure, even architectonic (church, office, halls, including the painter Titorelli's studio), are joined, constituting one single unit, one single space belonging to the court. The distorted, symbolic, or surrealistic images in *The Trial* almost always correspond to defined deliriums, dreams, fevers, or hallucinations, motivated as a consequence of pneumonia and not an execution at the hands of the court's executioners, or a way to show that the court and the judge are of this world as well as divine. We recall that Joseph K. feels ill, under the weather, goes out by necessity sent by the bank's president to meet with an Italian client in a church. Before he enters K. gets soaking wet, which, along with the cold temperature and the long wait in the cathedral, could have caused the pneumonia which made him hallucinate the visions presented to him during the scene of the judgment of his own life before those two strange executioners whom K. sees like old comedians from the opera.

The discovery—or at least the most interesting rediscovery from the point of view of the theater—concerning this stage adaptation of the novel is related to K.'s dialogues. In the Barrault-Gide version, the authors limit themselves to the texts which in the novel are attributed to Joseph K. In his version, Orson Welles follows the same procedure, only that on occasion he invents dialogues and situations (mainly at the end) that are not in the novel in order thereby to give his own particular anarchist interpretation.

The European film "The Trial" (1993) by David Jones surprised me greatly because of its proximity to the atmosphere described by Kafka; those rooftops and old buildings and nineteenth-century balconies reminded me a great deal of the novel, to which the film is faithful even, for example, in the disgusting stream that issues from one of the buildings near the painter's house. Also, this film captures the elegant atmosphere in which K. and Dr. Huld evolve.

This film is of an acute pathos clear as the light of day that needs neither grandiloquence nor gloom. It is a fine pathos which without a doubt has influenced Harold Pinter with all his experience. Nevertheless, solemnity and lack of humor persist, even in the casting of the actor, too much of a suitor, too handsome, and as a character too serene, too unfailingly self-confident. Confidence of course is expected by the bank manager, who requires that K. justify his innocence on two occasions. There is no self-judgment; punishment comes only from the outside, from the State, from life, from God, or from destiny. Once more, Joseph K. is a hero, a victim.

The contribution of the present theatrical version to the adaptations of *The Trial* consists in adding to Joseph K.'s dialogues comments that the narrator sometimes makes. These enrich the dialogues enormously. They become more theatrical and profuse, and much more comic, maintaining an oftentimes playful and critical spirit, eliminating Kafka's descriptions of what the character justly lacks.

Something similar happens with the rest of the characters. Sometimes I found phrases or events in other passages that do not belong to a particular scene but that I considered fundamental since they added elements that could clarify and even further deepen the situation, the environment of the character Joseph K., and the essential intentions of the novel. That is the case, for instance, with the signs placed in the court: "Generally our trials have foregone conclusions," and "Not only is ignorance of the law condemned, but so is innocence." These phrases that are mentioned in other chapters were extracted and placed in the judgment scene. Thus, I thought they were significant since they signaled ideas that clarify and illustrate the general spirit of the subject and the author's intentions.

Authority is the same, and the authorities all look alike, as Joseph K. reminds us in the scene with the attorney Huld, seeing his resemblance to the presiding judge. Because of this, I have suggested using the same actor to play all the roles of authority, including the priest in the cathedral.

Comic Kafka

A few months after finishing the adaptation "The Comic Trial of Joseph K." I came across a book by Gilles Deleuze and Felix Guattari. It was most gratifying to see agreement with my point of view in their radical phrases: "Only two principles to ally with Kafka: he is an author who laughs, profoundly content, with joy in life, in spite of his declarations of clowning..." At least five years earlier I had discovered this for myself.

I was even happier when I found out that I wasn't alone in my discovery. After the performance, which I directed and in which I performed the role of the comic Joseph K., the Guatemalan-Mexican writer Augusto Monterroso, a man with a fine sense of humor indeed, confessed to me that he had been thinking along the same lines for quite some time, and to prove this (as if it were necessary) he showed me the evidence, a book he had published in 1972 where he discusses Kafka's humor. Then I was no longer surprised but surely most joyful at seeing the cinematic work of the Kafkaesque Woody Allen in *Shadows and Fog*, where the filmmaker boasts of his vast knowledge of the humorous works of Franz Kafka.

As a well cultured man of his epoch, the man from Prague must have known (and I even dare to assert that he enjoyed) the fundamental creation of the beginning of the twentieth century, the cinematograph, the comic silent cinema. Surprisingly, there is almost a visual connection that exists between the comic situations presented in Kafka's novel and those proposed by the movies of the period. On numerous occasions even the "gag" (visual humor) intervenes, like those of Chaplin and Keaton, as in the court's offices when the front desk employee uses a cane to open a small skylight for fresh air, and instead a full load of dust falls "right on top of K.'s head," so that they have to close it right back. Another example is the notorious relationship between the personality of the ridiculous, lordly Joseph K. and the figure and attitudes of Charlie Chase, which was why in our staged presentation we decided to put prescription glasses on the young K., and the slight resemblance to Oliver Hardy.

It seems that silent films influenced the work of Franz Kafka the way that the movies of Laurel and Hardy have been said to have influenced the works of Samuel Beckett, especially in *Waiting for Godot* (as I was able to verify in a great documentary for American television which illustrated the subject), or the well-known influence of the dialogues of the Marx brothers on the entire theater of the absurd.

Political Kafka

In *Kafka, Toward a Minor Literature* (referring to a literature of minorities, not for minorities), Gilles Deleuze and Felix Guattari maintain that "All Kafka is comic, all Kafka is political." At least this is another way to understand Kafka's work, politics understood in its widest sense.

Kafka "is from beginning to end a political author, a fortune-teller of the future world because he has two poles to unite in a totally new device: far from being a writer isolated in his bedroom, his bedroom serves him for a double flowing, that of a bureaucracy of a very promising time to come, connected to real devices that are being created; and that of a nomad that runs away in the most contemporary style, that connects with socialism, anarchism, social movements."

This does not mean that the intentions of the writer stop there. Nevertheless, a pointed look into Kafka's work will show us his preocuppations with the abusive and ridiculous attitudes of authority and a concern for the suffering as well as the misery of others (one need only recall his interest in the nursery which Felice used to attend, and his intention even to become a soldier during the war. In truth this interest would only be temporary as he would tirelessly declare his only interest to be in literature, an attitude which, however, produced in him a great deal of guilt).

I had a reason to personify the narrator of the novel as an omnipresent craftsman. Aside from telling the story, he offers a permanent critique (no humor without criticism) of those important gentlemen and bank employees, starting with the boss (who pats his employees on their backs like cows, so that they will produce more milk), as well as all the repugnant bureaucratic machinery of legal authority. Thus, the comment the narrator makes when K. is going to visit the painter Titorelli, who lives in a poor neighborhood on the outskirts of the city, diametrically opposite the court's offices: "there existed a neighborhood even poorer than that surrounding the tribunals; the houses were much more sordid." The narrator is talking about the patio of the housing complex, where a yellowish substance that makes the rats run away issues from a hole in the wall. "At the foot of the stairs, face down on the floor, there was a baby crying, but the crying could hardly be heard because of the noise coming from the tin shop on the other side of the corridor from the entrance. Inside, three apprentices gathered around an object which they wouldn't stop beating with their hammers. A large aluminum sheet hanging from the wall casts a pale light on the two men, illuminating their faces and work aprons." He continues, "to all this picture K. gave only a swift look, interested as he was in his own personal affairs."

Time and Place

In the hand program of our staging of "The Comic Trial of Joseph K." I wrote that during my adolescence the literature of Franz Kafka aroused the same terror as the Frankenstein movie had during my childhood. To think that the human being would live eternally in a frightful world, without any order, or with a perverse order and sense, gave me long nights of insomnia and anguish, just as the wonderful movie monster that only now seems to me full of tenderness as interpreted by Boris Karloff. By substituting Joseph K. in a given social context, in the city of Prague at the beginning of the century, much of the abstract terror disappeared for me and made me see the characters of the novel as much less terrible. If the circumstances and characteristics surrounding K. were susceptible of transformation, the anguish he suffers would be less terrifying.

It is undisputable that Kafka's genius makes us feel the circumstances as absolute. We have the impression that the human being and his miserable condition will never change, nor will his relationship with authority, an exaggerated perception, at times in great part moved by an abusive and impulsive father (according to Franz Kafka, since in his pictures we have the impression of a tender, even nice old man). If this frightening image of the world that surrounds us is well placed, in a mature way and in concrete circumstances, the childish vision of terror disappears, allowing comedy to occur. The truth is that the "Kafkaesque" situations in which we continuously see ourselves involved in the offices of bureaucracy keep on making us experience feelings of impotence; we feel controlled by superior authoritarian forces that manipulate our lives. At least we know that there are real officers who are responsible for our misfortune and that, nevertheless, their attitudes, though comical, are able to provoke attacks of laughter as when Kafka regales Felice to prove to her that he knows how to laugh. This possibly deliberate confusion on Franz's part between father, bureaucrat, and God, once disentangled, makes us feel less miserable. At least we may hope to bring about change towards a more authentic participation, call it democratic. This has been one of the intentions of the current adaptation: to place Joseph K. in a specific context, in a specific time, and to insist that this alteration is not a fallacy but at least a possible utopia.

Ethical Judgment

But although the critique he directs at the financial, juridical, and political bureaucracy is ferocious, no less so is the one Franz Kafka directs at himself, at his own behavior. Here we have an ethical self-judgment of Joseph K. in which Franz Kafka judges himself, finds himself guilty, and condemns himself for being arrogant, egocentric, frivolous, only interested in his own convenience, and so on.

It is important to point out this fundamental aspect, since it is most common to consider K. an innocent victim of the world, the system, the bureaucracy, and so on, when in reality the lordly, selfish, and vain Joseph K. deserves, according to Kafka, if not all then most of what happens to him. Among other options, *The Trial* is a judgment in which, on his thirtieth birthday, Kafka judges himself, finds himself full of defects, and exactly one year later he declares himself guilty, he repents painfully of all frivolity and the lack of compromise in which he has lived, and he sentences himself to die — perhaps of the pulmonary illness that finished him off.

Felice Bauer

Clearly some of Kafka's female characters are based on the person of Felice Bauer, Kafka's fiancée with whom he exchanged obsessive letters, and it seems evident that the character of Fraulein Bürstner has much in common with Felice. Even her initials are the same, and they have the same profession (secretary) and similar tastes, such as a joy in attending the theater. Because of this I was always irritated by the Wellesian vision of this character. In his film Orson Welles conceives F. B. as a vulgar drunken prostitute, a totally idiosyncratic conception. It is clear that Joseph K. is a hypocrite or jealous and is disturbed by the open attitude of the overly liberal Miss Bürstner, whom he has seen at night coming out of theaters accompanied by different men each time. This in no way means that we are talking about a prostitute. On the contrary, there is enough evidence to demonstrate that Franz admired the practical and liberal attitudes of a modern woman without complications that attracted him to Felice. Kafka describes her as "a happy, healthy, and self-confident girl." But her modest position of secretary and her night walks to the theater are subjects of scorn and severe criticism on the part of Joseph K. in spite of his interest in her; he could even have fallen in love with her. But K. does not dare to recognize and to acknowledge his interest in her although he reveals it on numerous occasions.

The lack of definition in the structure of *The Trial* is also surprising. It seems that Franz Kafka never got to set the sequence of these chapters. One wonders why he left us a legacy of quite dispersed chapters that never quite conclude. Here we have a splendid example of dramatic structure that modern filmmakers would envy—sections that are never defined but that leave the door open for a new version or a fresh change. Kafka wouldn't know in what order to put the chapters, or if he even wanted to order them; nevertheless, Kafka knew exactly what he was doing and finished up, as if he was unable to make the selection either deliberately or for lack of time. "Freedom is the choice of the necessity," as Octavio Paz observes in a poem. Kafka does not want to be free, or he cannot be free. Joseph K. does not choose, nor does Kafka. "If you don't marry me you'll be sorry, and if you marry me you'll be sorry as well," suggests Kafka in a letter to Felice. Why choose if there is no solution, of any kind, for the human being? Contrary to what is commonly believed, he who doesn't choose is not free, but only he who is capable of choosing. Only compromise can offer freedom, or as Goethe says, "Life is a door that opens outwards." Neither Kafka nor K. could open it, although both were capable of knowing it and communicating it.

Kafka: Hope and Despair

Thus, the interesting vision of Deleuze and Guattari: "Only one thing bothers Kafka and makes him furious; he's indignant when treated as an intimate writer, who finds refuge in literature, author of solitude, of guilt, of inner suffering. Thus, guilt is all his because he has lifted all this . . . to advance into the trap and for humor. . . . It is for the same stupid reasons that one has been wanting to see solely, I think, in Kafka's literature, a refuge separate from life and also . . . anguish, the stamp of impotence and guilt, the sign of a sad inner tragedy." (p. 64) The fact is that Kafka is much more than this. Popular wisdom admonishes that "a sad saint is a poor saint." But Kafka was not a sad saint. He was a man whom his friends identified as young, joyful, and carefree, who knew how to laugh. To identify him only as a sad and above all hopeless being is another one of the myths that this work pretends to demolish. Kafka, like all prophets, is a man full of rage and pain, but, in spite of all commonplaces, like all prophets of desperation he is a man full of love for mankind, with hope in humanity. From him I have received the most hopeful and desolate phrase I have ever heard; it is a phrase from his diary: "Even if there is no redemption in this world, we should all live as if there were." It is the most beautiful example I have found of human dignity.

One has the idea that prophets like Kafka, Beckett, or Herman Melville are lonely men who hate humanity. These critics of the human condition! "Go back to your sewer to rub your bellies!" anathematizes the prophet Samuel Beckett. If this is the final destiny of humanity, we should all disappear under the explosion of an atomic bomb. What will happen after one's departure, when the rich, the vegetation, the animals have disappeared and when we have no more light, narcotics, uppers, or downers? And at our own demise, when we won't have erections and our lovers have long died loveless of abandonment, when victimized by the AIDS virus or cancer we finally end bald and toothless, our ideals? In a similar but distinct way we are incriminated by Melville's Bartleby, the saddest story in literature, when he warns us that in a mercantilized world, manipulated by a hypocritical, convenient, and mediocre religion, man's life lacks sense; it is like a letter that never reaches its addressee. It seems that these *poètes maudites* would only feel scorn for humanity. Nevertheless, for these hopeless men there is an exit, always that of solidarity and love for people, the same exit that the bureaucrats of the 1940s couldn't find, those who condemned Kafka as a writer of a decadent literature, when he talked about a different kind of person, who refused to die like a dog, and who only wished to maintain, until the end, his serenity of mind and his capacity of analysis, his dignity, his only weapon, his bastion and pride, although inexorable logic would not stop a man who loves life and wants to keep on living. In his diary that man opened a door for mankind, for people in the middle of a rainfall: "Strong rain," said Franz in his diary; "face the rain. Let its fierce beating soak you. Slip through the water that means to drag you down. But in spite of everything, resist. Wait standing for the sun that enters suddenly and endlessly in torrents."

Franz Kafka, 1883-1924, forty-one years old, was a man who loved life and knew how to laugh. The most beautiful page of Max Brod's book about Kafka is when he tells how the audience laughed irresistibly at a reading of the first chapter of *The Trial*.

Héctor Ortega's stage version of Franz Kafka's *The Trial* supposes some kind of equation of syllogisms among three terms.

Hugo Hiriart

The first term is the prudent writer who lived in Prague, that is to say, Kafka the persona. The second term is the actor and political animal who lives in Mexico, that is to say, Héctor Ortega. And these two together give the kafkaesque to the theater piece.

Like Ramón López Velarde, Kafka was a man tragically divided. He was attracted to marriage, to family life, to gearing into society, but he knew that many times family is nothing more than an inferno, and a very obstructing inferno for the work of a writer. But what is the alternative? Kafka, like López Velarde, compared the bachelor to a phantom: a being who doesn't exist entirely, who drowns in monologues, in silence, in solitude. What can be done? Nothing. Being single is bad, but being married is also bad, perhaps even worse. What do we do then? We write *The Trial*, a work that as is known was born of Kafka's break-up with Felice Bauer, for which he was judged. Within the Jewish community, divorce is permitted but not breaking up a marriage engagement, a grave thing. There is a reason for this; if you try and it doesn't work, this is very different from breaking up before you know whether a marriage works. Dissolving an engagement remains inexplicable and offensive, for which Kafka was accused and subjected to a trial. His novel was born of the artist's divided self, of his tragic disjunction.

The second term. Héctor Ortega is not a divided man. He possesses an amazing unity. Ortega is not only an actor of prodigious timing and expressiveness, which aligns him with the *commedia del'arte* that we all have enjoyed, but he is something more. He is reflective and preoccupied with society and politics, possessed of a strange severity and a very rare honesty in the small world of entertainment. His specialty is comedy.

Given these two terms we can ask ourselves: How does a complete and healthy man understand a divided and tragic man? How does Héctor Ortega understand Kafka? The answer to this question brings us to the "kafkaesque," the third term of our equation.

We hear of the kafkaesque. We hear it said, for example, that Mexico is a kafkaesque country. So we can ask ourselves, what is the kafkaesque? The narrative procedure of Kafka, whereof the kafkaesque is born (and there are other procedures, but we won't talk about those), consists of the following:

We narrate a scene with details, with precise realism, every detail, except one. The missing detail, the supressed detail, tints the other details with a strange tone of absurdity. For instance, a fat man comes to my house to see me. He talks about this and that. I describe him, and I tell what we talk about. Everything is fine, except that I don't know what this man wants. I have no idea why he came to see me. The fat man drinks his coffee and leaves. And that is kafkaesque: everything the fat man has done in my house takes on a flavor of absurdity.

The procedure is underscored when something is clearly contradicted. For example, a door is built never to be opened. The supression of the "what for?" creates, in these cases, a mental dead-end. The connection here with politics and social life is immediate. For instance, all the public telephones are changed so they will only take cards, but the cards are not made, or they become scarce, like a collector's item, or they are not distributed. This also creates a mental dead-end.

What does this tell us? Two things. The kafkaesque appears when the steps to get to something are inverted, altered, or multiplied senselessly and do not indicate in any way how to get there with those steps or where they lead. Second, the kafkaesque always implies secrecy, something we wish to know that we don't know, something that others know and we don't. And from secrecy comes power: the fat man who comes home to see me, in the given example, has power over me because he knows what he came for and I don't know.

So there are three phases: the steps to get to something are inverted, the inversion engenders secrecy, and secrecy generates a strategy of power according to which one knows secret commands and another who doesn't know can only be silent and obedient.

Now, it has been said, and rightly so, that in all of Kafka the strength and intelligence came from his extreme mildness: since he never used power, he was infinitely sensitive to how power was inflicted upon him, and he could describe it like no one else could, with extraordinary precision.

Kafka was not political. His journal entry of August 12, 1914, says: Germany declared war on Russia (semicolon) this afternoon I'm going to swimming class. But Ortega is interested in social and political life. That is why in his adaptation of Kafka's novel he understood the political sense of Kafka in the way I have set it out. In this fashion, the first note of the kafkaesque, according to Ortega, is that what for Kafka is inner suffocation, interior judgment, is amplified to a social context and becomes political suffocation and aberration of social life. And let's say that this is the general tendency: the complete man tends to transform the inner and personal drama into something external and universal, more visible and clear, and also more manageable, because a distinctive sign of the undivided person is that he not only wants to understand but to fight as well. What is there to do? What is there to do? is his question.

The second note of the kafkaesque according to Ortega is humor. We said that in Kafka's narrative procedure suppression of a detail generates the absurd. This absurd is by all means comic. The humor is always based on the absurd. We should not forget that the plays of Ionesco, prototype of the theater of the absurd, are comedies (Martin Esslin enlarged the notion of the theater of the absurd to include, for example, a bullfighter as a deviation of this theater).

Many have attempted to suppress the humor of the kafkaesque, Orson Welles, for example, in his film "The Trial." The result is sinister but always with a heavy dose of tedium. The tedium comes from the fact that in the senseless there cannot be suspense of any kind. There is not the "and then" and "the next" of good story-telling. The senseless is static; it cannot be developed, and it's all done, in the end, heavily and solemnly. But this is betraying Kafka. Nobody is less solemn than Kafka, because in solemnity there will always be strategies of power and, as we saw, Kafka was the mild one, he who cautiously evaded all forms of personal power.

To our good fortune, neither is Héctor Ortega solemn, and his reading of the kafkaesque coincides in this point of humor with readings given by Kafka himself. In Ortega's version, Kafka resembles Laurel and Hardy, Chaplin, and Buster Keaton. And this is an enormous praise for Ortega, because these masters achieved in the art of entertainment the masterpieces of broadest reach, works that delighted T.S. Eliot and Beckett—demanding spectators— but that also appeal to an illiterate Chinese child. More you cannot ask in the field of art.

I've gone too far, and I don't know if I'm speaking objectively any longer, or only with the admiration and warm feelings that I have for Héctor Ortega. Both ways of speaking are, in this case, equally good.

Kafka Unveiled

Manuel Flores

"I was leafing through a magazine while waiting for Joseph K., my beagle, to emerge from his regular Tuesday fifty-minute hour with a Park Avenue therapist—a Jungian veterinarian who, for fifty dollars per session, labors valiantly to convince him that jowls are not a social drawback," notes Woody Allen in the opening lines of his story "Yes, But Can the Steam Engine Do This?" from his book *Getting Even* included in *The Complete Prose of Woody Allen* (1991; p. 177). Needless to say, these lines set the tone of great humor that prevails throughout the story. Of course these lines could very well refer not only to Kafka's depressive relation with the society of his time but to the sometimes absurdist quality of his literature. Their irony reminds us that Kafka's testimony is much more than metaphysics. It is humor. There is an even clearer example of how Allen conceives, uses, and inspires his own works by using elements from Kafka's work, and for this specific example some elements of *The Trial* (the passage where the priest narrates the story of the peasant, the door, and the guardian of the law). Allen creates a short story, a parody of this passage in his story "Two Parables," where he begins:

> A man approaches a palace. Its only entrance is guarded by some fierce Huns who will only let a man named Julius enter. The man tries to bribe the guards by offering them a year's supply of choice chicken parts. They neither scorn his offer nor accept it, but merely take his nose and twist it till it looks like a Molly screw. The man says it is imperative that he enters the palace because he is bringing the emperor a change of underwear. When the guards still refuse, the man begins to Charleston. They seem to enjoy his dancing but soon become morose

over the treatment of the Navajos by the federal government. Out of breath, the man collapses. He dies, never having seen the emperor and owing the Steinway people sixty dollars on a piano he had rented from them in August. (p. 172)

Woody Allen also captures the spirit of Kafka's novel in his film "Shadows and Fog," where the essence of the kafkaesque is a constant delight. Of course Woody Allen was not the first to identify the humor in Kafka's works, or in the situations and characters of *The Trial*. There have been others (but not very many), and the reason could be related to the capital importance of Kafka in modern literature, the weight he has among us mortal writers, and the fact that it is safer to stick to an intellectually and socially accepted conception of Kafka's metaphysics. Kafka's literature is a world unto itself and a very complete one at that, in which laughter is necessarily just one of the elements.

In this respect, another author who gets a good laugh from Kafka's writings is Salman Rushdie in his collection of essays *Imaginary Homelands* (1991. "The Location of Brazil" refers to Terry Gilliam's film "Brazil." Rushdie pretends to establish the location and time of the story:

> So are we to say that this is a film that is somehow located in a song? Well, there's an ironic sense in which that might be true. The lush innocence of the old tune, when set against Gilliam's tale of State terror, does indeed embody much of the film's spirit, a combination, as Gilliam has said, of Franz Kafka and Frank Capra. (p. 119)

Rushdie goes on to differentiate the British and American approaches to comedy, the former based on the starting-point question "Wouldn't it be funny if . . . ?" and the latter beginning with the question "Isn't funny that . . . ?" He ends up pointing out Kafka as a key to the film's method of comedy:

> One of the keys to his (Gilliam's) method is Kafka. A story like "Metamorphosis" appears, at first glance, to fall into the "British" camp: wouldn't it be funny if Gregor Samsa woke up one morning to find himself metamorphosed into a giant insect? But in fact it derives its (very black) humor from a rather more serious question: Isn't funny that a man's family reacts with fear, embarrassment, shame, love, boredom and relief when the son of the house becomes something they do not understand, suffers terribly and finally dies? The humor in "Brazil" is similarly black ... And like Kafka, it uses "surface" techniques of the Absurdist.... (p. 124)

More recently I came across the book *Introducing Kafka* (1994) by David Zane Mairowitz and illustrated by the world's leading underground comic artist, Robert Crumb. Aside from the darkly humorous drawings, we find a wise and intelligent vision of Kafka's life and works by Mairowitz.

> No writer of our time, and probably none since Shakespeare, has been so widely over-interpreted and pigeon-holed. Jean-Paul Sartre claimed him for Existentialism, Camus saw him as an absurdist, his life-long friend and editor, Max Brod, convinced several generations of scholars that his parables were part of an elaborate quest for an unreachable God.
> Because his novels *The Trial* and *The Castle* deal with the inaccessibility of higher authority, "Kafkaesque" has come to be associated with the faceless bureaucratic infrastructure which the highly efficient Austro Hungarian Empire bequeathed the Western world. In any case, it is an adjective that takes on almost mythic proportions in our time, irrevocably tied to fantasies of doom and gloom, ignoring the intricate Jewish Joke that weaves itself through the bulk of Kafka's work. ... But sooner or later, even the most hateful of Jewish Self-Hatreds has to turn around and laugh at himself. In Kafka, the duality of dark melancholy and hilarious self-abasement is nearly always at work. "Kafkaesque" is usually swollen with notions of terror and bitter anguish. But Kafka's stories, however grim, are nearly always also ... FUNNY. (pp. 5, 25)

About *The Trial* specifically, Mairowitz notes:

> Begun in 1914, this is probably his best-known book, and certainly provides the basis for the popular notion of "Kafkaesque." What the story demonstrates most clearly about Kafka-the-Night-Writer is the precision, the humor and luck of overt emotion with which he can describe all his own nightmares.... When Kafka read passages from *The Trial* out loud to his friends, he is reported to have laughed uncontrollably. (pp. 88, 95)

These last lines of Mairowitz coincide with something I read from the renowned Guatemalan writer Augusto Monterroso noted in his book *La letra E* (1987) about a visit he made to an exhibition entitled "A la recherche de Franz Kafka" in the Jewish Art Museum of Prague:

> Lost this (the exhibition), naturally, in one of the streets of more difficult access of this city. Frustrating from beginning to end. A few editions, well known, in French; the conceived views of Prague, bad paintings and drawings, inspired (per se) without a doubt in the now traditional bad reading of Kafka, directed mildly to find symbols of the anguish of our time, of course, even in the passages of his novels in which Kafka had more fun writing. (p. 30)

Kafka the humorist, the joker, amused himself writing his stories, and I'm sure that in the back of his mind there was always the intention of entertaining others, his readers, his listeners, to make them think but also to make them laugh. I believe that we seek in the mirror of Kafka's literature a reflection of ourselves, our miseries, and that is what we want (and perhaps need) to see to be able to punish and redeem ourselves from our sins, but for all of those neurotic and claustrophobic readers of Kafka, within the dark alleys and false doors of his literature there is an exit, a not so well hidden door, and the key to this door is humor, but we seem whether or not intentionally to avoid looking at it.

Recently I read "Testaments Betrayed" (1995) by novelist

92   Kafka Unveiled

Milan Kundera. This is an essay in nine parts, dominated by Kundera's meditations on bad readings and misconceptions of Kafka and his works. Kafka left us a vast universe of wisdom and poetry, a profound knowledge of the human spirit, but also a painful diagram of the human condition. Not knowing what to do with the unknown and unfamiliar, as well as with the divine, we have inevitably betrayed the inheritance. The first time this testament was betrayed was when, against the author's wishes, his closest friend, Max Brod, published his manuscripts. Brod then betrayed Kafka again when, according to Kundera, not fully understanidng Kafka's works he censored complete lines of these manuscripts in order to make them reflect his, Brod's, own perception of the author and his works, and of course by this he betrayed humanity in general by depriving future generations of readers of the Kafka's true and complete words. The third time Kafka's testament was betrayed was when a limited group of artists and intellectuals with the power to disseminate their opinions through Europe found in Kafka's works only a banner to manifest the oppression and dehumanization they were experiencing during the first half of the century. Then came another betrayal, one last assault against the monumental figure, the translations. These were done in a way that reflect primarily the translator's own understanding of Kafka more through interpretation than through translating, shamelessly limiting the author, to our own loss.

Through the lens of Kundera's insights, the image of Kafka takes on a different meaning, signaling and condemning those responsible for some of the bad readings and misconceptions of the Polish author. Kundera points to the causes which he believes brought about this catastrophe.

> People first read Kafka with a tragic expression on their faces. Then they heard that when Kafka read the first chapter of *The Trial* to his friends, he made them all laugh. Thereupon readers started forcing themselves to laugh too, but without knowing exactly why. What actually is so funny in this chapter? K.'s

behavior. But what is comic about his behavior? (p. 205)

This paragraph struck me most, not only because it serves the purpose of this research but because it validates with the best of intentions Kundera's comments on Kafka's comedy. Beginning the second part of his essay entitled "The Castrating Shadow of Saint Garta," Kundera says:

> Young Karl Rossmann (the protagonist of *Amerika*) is put out of the parental home and sent to America because of his unfortunate sexual mishap with a housemaid ... This minor copulation is the cause of everything to follow in the novel. Realizing that our destiny is determined by something utterly trivial is depressing. But any revelations of some unexpected triviality is a source of comedy as well. *Post coitum omne animal triste.* Kafka was the first to describe the comic side of that sadness.
>
> The comic side of sex: an idea unacceptable to puritans and neolibertines both. I think of D. H. Lawrence, that bard of Eros, that evangelist of coition, who, in *Lady Chatterly's Lover*, tried to rehabilitate sex by making it lyrical. But lyrical sex is even more ridiculous than the lyrical sentimentality of the last century.
>
> The erotic gem of *Amerika* is Brunelda. She fascinated Federico Fellini. For a long time, he dreamed of making a film of *Amerika,* and in his *Intervista* there is a scene that shows the casting for this dream project: a bunch of incredible candidates turn out for the role of Brunelda, women Fellini had picked with the exuberant delight he was known for. (But I say it again: that exuberance is the same as Kafka's. For Kafka did not *suffer* for us! He *enjoyed* himself for us!) ... What is new about this portrait of massive ugliness is that it is alluring; morbidly alluring, ridiculously alluring, but still alluring; Brunelda is a monster of sex on the borderline between the repugnant and the exciting, and men's admiring cries are not only comic (they *are* comic, to be sure, sex *is* comic!) (46, 47, 48) ... From the first lines, the spirit of playful parody generates an imaginary world where nothing is completely plausible and everything is a little comical. ... So it is through parodic playing (playing with clichés) that Kafka first set out the greatest theme, that of the labyrinthine social organizations where man loses his way and

94   Kafka Unveiled

proceeds to his ruin. (Genetically speaking: the comical mechanism of the uncle's desk is the ancestor of the terrifying castle administration.) (81, 82).

Kundera goes on to mention another scene from Chapter 12 of *the Castle,* involving K., Frieda, and the two assistants camping:

> ... this scene with its enormous comic poetry (which should head the list in an anthology of modernism in novel) ...He (Kafka) managed to solve this enormous puzzle. He cut a breach in the wall of plausibility; the breach through which many others followed him, each in his own way: Fellini, Márquez, Fuentes, Rushdie. And others, others. To hell with Saint Garta! His castrating shadow has blocked our view of one of the novel's greatest poets of all time. (52, 53)

Kafka, like Cervantes, has transcended the world and literature. The characters they once created have abandoned the pages to which they were first destined and gone out to Broadway, the cinema, have turned into sculpted stones, into musical notes. But perhaps, as the great novelist Carlos Fuentes once pointed out, referring to the painted version of literature, Picasso's interpretation of Don Quixote was the closest version, the most faithful replica of Cervantes's masterpiece he had ever encountered, since Picassos' drawing was composed only of black ink, the essensial element of the written word, letters turned to image.

Kafka as well has been the subject of all manner of interpretation whether on stage, the big screen, or in the visual arts. Here the definitive interpretation is by the outstanding talent of another great artist, José Luis Cuevas, who has captured in his drawings of Kafka's world the essence of the human condition that the author envisioned, the absurdist thus true spirit of what the writer left on paper to haunt and to amuse us. Cuevas's always extraordinary paintings and drawings reflect the profound influence of the kafkaesque on the Mexican artist. It seems appropriate, then, to remember that Max Brod, according to Cuevas, named him in his testament the rightful illustrator of Kafka (with the only restriction of not illustrating the insect into which Gregor Samsa turns in "The Metamorphosis," since Kafka never wished to mention the specific kind of insect in the story), and Cuevas has respected that wish. In Cuevas, Brod found a close, even intimate understanding of Kafka's journey among us and recognized in the Mexican artist the authenticity of his own reflections about the author's legacy to humanity.

In his book *En Torno a Cuevas,* Cuevas the painter/author, talking about Buster Keaton, comments:

> ... Keaton laughed loud, and the public laughed with him. He laughed mainly at his own treason, since the great comedian, for money, for hunger, indulged himself in an expression that did not belong to him. The laughter of Keaton impressed me profoundly. [...] I don't know exactly how, but I embodied this experience in my illustrations of Kafka. (p. 54)

Finally, as I end this a memory from my past comes to mind, when I was a young child and saw Leonardo Da Vinci's "Mona Lisa" for the first time. I was captivated and intrigued by her enigmatic smile. Much had been said about a "secret" she was hiding behind her smile, but what was she hiding? Like the rest of humanity, I questioned myself. Back then there was no answer. I never forgot her smile, nor the question that lay on the soft lines of her lips. It wasn't until many years later that I saw on television a scientific study done on this masterpiece; through advanced technology they pretended to uncover the mysterious secret of her smile, superimposing a picture of a smiling Da Vinci himself on the face of the Mona Lisa. The proportions of both their faces — eyes, noses, and the lines of their smiles — coincided, so what they thought they had discovered was truly a self-portrait of Da Vinci himself hidden beneath her smile. The secret had been

96   *Kafka Unveiled*

unveiled, and I was satisfied, thinking that Da Vinci had played a good joke on us that had lasted all these many years. As an adolescent when I first discovered Kafka I also saw a well-known picture of the author wearing a discrete smile which I found enigmatic and not so well concealed as Mona Lisa's. This smile immediately questioned me. What is it hiding? What is it hiding? I keep asking myself, but perhaps I shall ask no more.

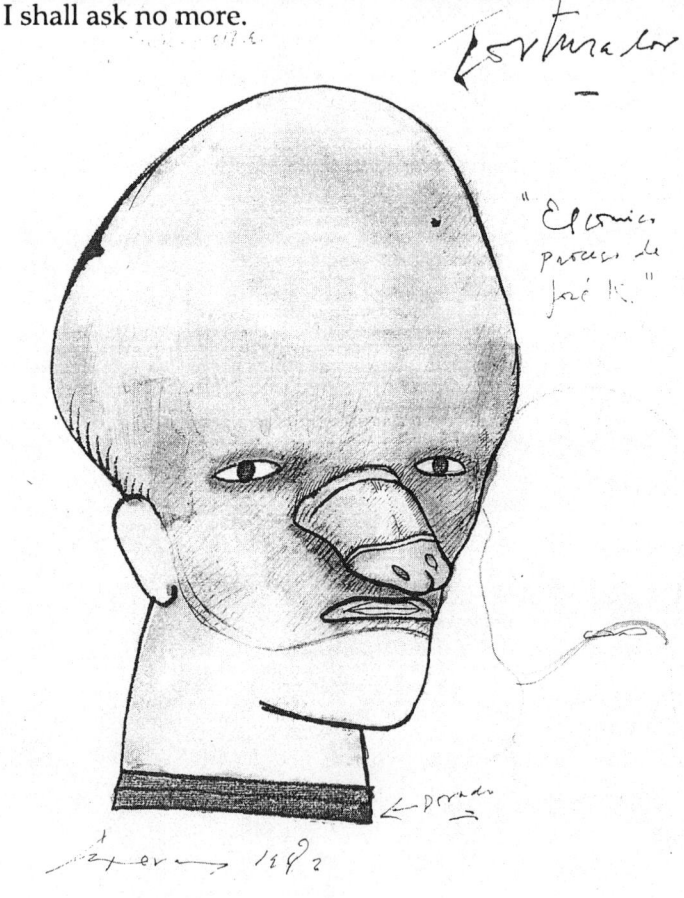

Figure 8. "Whipper." José Luis Cuevas. 1982.

Kafka's Humor: The Castle Jester

D. Emily Hicks

Humor, The Good City, Democracy, and Justice

Although dispute exists over a quote commonly attributed to Franz Kafka—there is "abundance of hope, but none for us"—there *is* agreement that he found even his most tragic work extremely funny.[1] In this essay, I will look at humor in Franz Kafka's work in relation to the analysis of Kafka by Gilles Deleuze and Felix Guattari. I will analyze the novels *The Castle*, *America*, and *The Trial*, and several short stories, including "The Judgment," "Metamorphosis," "In the Penal Colony," "A Hunger Artist," "The Bucket Rider," "The Truth About Sancho Panza," "The Great Wall of China," and "Investigations of a Dog." The text that most succinctly clarifies the painful core of the humor in Kafka is found in "Letter to the Father." I hope to show that in each example of Kafka's humor, an absurd, extreme reaction follows an innocent act. The arbitrariness and "injustice" of the "punishment" never fit the crime, yet the "punishment" is accepted. It is in the narrator's deadpan delivery of each of these incidents of "injustice" that one aspect of the humor is generated. The humorous and the human are linked through pathos in Kafka's work. It is a humor filled with pain, which the reader of *Don Quijote* may have experienced. As we laugh at Don Quijote's mishaps, we are drawn to his idealism and the social critique it implies. As we laugh at Sancho Panza's unwillingness, at least at first, to speculate about alternatives to the given social order, it is a poignant laughter, because we understand that Sancho Panza does not have the luxury to philosophize. However, while Don Quijote dies believing that he had been deluded by reading novels, K., in *The Trial*, dies believing that he has done the right thing in firing his lawyer. Of course, Kafka has his own reading of Sancho Panza: in "The Truth About Sancho Panza," he reveals Don Quijote to be a creation of Sancho Panza, who follows his adventures with great amusement. Here we see how the dismantling of assemblages and humor converge. In the third notebook of Kafka's *The Blue Octavo Notebooks*, the author writes, "Don Quixote's misfortune is not his imagination, but Sancho Panza." (15) A few days later, in the same notebook, he writes:

> One of the most important quixotic acts, more obtrusive than fighting the windmill, is: suicide. The dead Don Quixote wants to kill the Dead Don Quixote; in order to kill, however, he needs a place that is alive, and this he searches for with his sword, both ceaselessly and in vain. Engaged in this occupation the two dead men, inextricably interlocked and positively bouncing with life, go somersaulting away down the ages. (18)

To focus on humor in its usual sense is to depoliticize the discussion of Kafka's work; therefore, I will discuss humor as it relates to Kafka's Nietzschean affirmation of life and his hope for and faith in democracy, despite all the negativity and despair in his work. His is not a naive view of democracy nor is it a view of democracy based on slavery in which slaves and women have no voice. In one of the deleted passages of *The Trial*, he writes: "As you know, employees always know more than their employers." ("The Passages Deleted by the Author p. 12," *Kafka* 258) Rather, Kafka's view of democracy is a profound understanding of a distinction Antonio Negri makes in Spinoza's work, a distinction between power and Power (*potestas* and *potere*). Referring to Spinoza's logic, Michael Hardt, in his translator's foreword to *The Savage Anomaly: The Power of Spinoza's Metaphysics and Politics*, writes:

... aristocracy is a less limited form of government [in relation to the monarch] to the extent that the supreme Power, in the form of a council, is more fully constituted by the multitude. Democratic government is the final point of this process, but unfortunately, Spinoza died before finishing this section [of his work] ... Democracy is to be the absolute, unlimited form of government, because in it the supreme Power is fully constituted by the power of the multitude. Spinoza's democracy is to be animated by a constituent Power, a dynamic form of popular authority. With this progression from monarchy through aristocracy to democracy, Spinoza moves from history to metaphysics, from Power to power. (xvi)

Upon what notion of being does Kafka base this affirmative view of life? What is the source of his strength when K., at the conclusion of *The Trial*, faces death? I argue that Kafka's conception of being is, as Negri describes Spinoza's, the product of humanism and Hebraic philosophy and that it is Spinozan; as Negri writes, "The conception of being in Spinoza ... is the conception of a powerful being, which knows no hierarchies, which knows only its own constitutive force." (11) This is the conception of being in Kafka that is revealed to us through humor. In the first step, Kafka describes the assemblages of power, by delineating their hierarchies; in the second step, he dismantles the assemblages of power, thereby offering to the reader the possibility of speculating about a being "which knows no hierarchies." We are implicated in the first step, because we are inscribed into both assemblages through the Law (death sentences, judgments) and through our sexual desire ("a machinic assemblage of bodies, passions and desires") — the Ship, the Hotel, the Castle, the Court. (*A Thousand Plateaus* 88) We are promised the possibility of freedom in the second step (the dismantling of the assemblage of desire and of "a collective assemblage of enunciations of acts and statements, of incorporeal transformations attributed to bodies"), because we are made to understand that we, as a part of being, cannot be completely contained by either of these machines. (88) That is, although we are caught in the desiring machine due to our own attractions, affects, and desires, and we are subject to the Law, we are also more than this, a supplement, a left-over, a trace. Let us imagine Spinoza's "good city" (a democracy) as a "city machine." Our affects are what inscribe us into this city. It is our ability to understand an emotinoal kabbalistic multi-centered geometry that paves a way towards pleasant encounters; it is in the fruitful encounter that the sad passions are overcome. Conversely, it is in the alienated encounter of bureaucracies that the sad passions keep the subject paralyzed. Now, we can imagne the one configuration of machinic assemblages that Kafka never describes, conspicuous by its absence, in which we would be free. In Kafka's short life, this city existed only in the minds of sympathetic readers.

Most distant from this utopian vision of life, the good city, is K.'s status in the village in *The Castle*. Today, K. might be compared to a guest worker in Europe or an undocumented worker in the U.S.-Mexico border region. He is sent for to work as a Land Surveyor, literally, to determine borders, but when he arrives, he is distrusted as a stranger, and there is confusion, perhaps even a mistake, about the position he is supposed to fill. Although the novel was never finished, according to what he told his friend Max Brod Kafka intended to write that K. was to die exhausted by his struggle, and that "word was to come that although K.'s legal claim to live in the village was not valid, yet, taking certain auxiliary circumstances into account, he was to be permitted to live and work there." (7) This is the situation of the undocumented worker, who is allowed to work in a country, at substandard wages, but he is not allowed citizenship. It is the situation of the Martinican described by Jean-François Lyotard in *The Differend*. Upon what basis does the Martinican make a legal claim about mistreatment? How can there be a shared legal code between the SS officer and the Jew? Like K. having to sleep in the school, undocumented workers have to work but do not have access to adequate housing. Because the undocumented worker is not a citizen and therefore does not have the legal protections of citizenship, there is little legal basis for a demand for better treatment. Whereas Marx focuses on the proletariat, a population with citizenship, Kafka analyzes the situation of the undocumented worker; both use irony in their critique of capitalism.

In a passage form "Letter to His Father," Kafka describes very succinctly "three worlds," which I will refer to as: 1) the first side of the assemblage — "a machine assemblage of bodies, actions, passions;" 2) a collective assemblage; and 3) the dismantling of two sides of the assemblage, a dismantling that emerges in a context of humor and which points to a vision of a world different from both the others — the good city. Kafka writes:

> Hence the world was for me divided into three parts: one in which I, the slave, lived under laws that had been invented only for me and which I could, I did not know why, never completely comply with; then a second world, which was infinitely remote from mine, in which you lived, concerned with the issuing of orders and with the annoyance about their not being obeyed; and finally a third world where everybody else lived happily and free from orders and from having to obey. (125)

The relationship of the non-citizen to the Law is analogous to the relationship of the subject to God in Spinoza and to the low-level functionary in the bureaucracies Kafka describes. How to find justice in such a system becomes a way for Kafka to examine larger issues, such as justice itself. In some stories, it is the narrator who cannot find justice, as is the case of K. in *The Castle*, and in others, it is a charcter with whom the narrator is in solidarity, as is the case of Karl and the Stoker.

A Deleuzo-Guattarian Approach

Although I will rely primarily on the analysis of Gilles Deleuze and Felix Guattari, I want to refer the reader to areas of research beyond the scope of this essay which add depth to my argument, namely, the Lacanian dichotomy between the symbolic and the imaginary, and the Freudian distinction between the conscious and the unconscious. In Lacan's essay "Tuché and the Automaton," the real comes through the father's unconscious in the form of the son crying, "Can't you see I'm burning?" In Freud's "The Uncanny" and in his work on humor, humor is generated through the slippage between the conscious and the unconscious. Each of these methods can help us to understand Kafka's humor as: 1) not funny; 2) social critique; and 3) linked to childhood experience. As indicated above, I will follow Antonio Negri's reading of Spinoza, that it is in the relation between forces that we can understand the positoning of the subject *vis-à-vis* the states.

Humor as Social Critique

In his humor, Kafka connects activities that are "a matter of course" with the bizarre, a juxtapositon analogous to biographical experiences that made no sense to him as a child, such as "the extraordinary territory of being carried outside to the *pavlatche*" after asking his father for a glass of water. ("Letter to His Father" 119) The *pavlatche* is "the Czech word for the long balcony in the inner courtyard in old houses in Prague." (119 note) This humor is generated by linking the mundane and the "innocent" to horrible, retaliatory reactions on the part of impersonal bureaucracies, as we see in the story "In the Penal Colony." In Kafka's humor, we find "exaggeration . . . to the point of absurdity," as Deluze and Guattari describe the "goal," "effect," and "procedure" behind Kafka's "move" in the letter to his father. The fact that the humor depends on at least two sets of referential codes, from both inside and outside of the sphere of cultural dominance, implies a social critique even when the progagonist, such as K., appears to defend the status quo. If we imagine the multi-centered kabbalistic geometry as digital, that is, able to access multiple centers in any order without being constrained by proceeding in a linear manner, then we may understand Kafka's humor as digital as well. There is not merely one "punch line" to each joke. Rather, there are resonances in multiple centers, assemblages, in response to the element of humor.

As Deleuze and Guattari define writing for Kafka, it "has a double function: to translate everything into assemblages and to dismantle the assemblages." (*Kafka* 47) In the dismantling we find Kafka's humor. However, in order to understand the humor, we must analyze, that is, break down into its constituent parts, the society he attacks. In Spinozan terms, through dismantling the assemblages he has first described Kafka generates humor that enables him to overcome the "sad passions." In this way, he leaves a position of passivity and moves into a position of activity. We see this process in *The Trial* when K. finally overcomes his sad passions and fires his lawyer. Taking action brings consequences, but at least K. is no longer paralyzed by indecision and depression. The chapter in which K. fires the lawyer is followed, in the Schocken edition, by "In the Cathedral" and then by the final chapter in which K. is killed. Of course, the order of the chapters is debated. In any event, in this order, the death of the protagonist follows, perhaps in response K.'s taking charge of his own life. However, I do not understand this to be a Hegelian point that Kafka is making, that the protagonist must, like the bondsperson, risk life in order to achieve mastery. Instead, I see Kafka making the point that once K. has overcome his emotional paralysis and is able to act, the consequences are less important than the process through which he went in overcoming his paralysis. Was K. not "dead" as he went to a job he hated, fearing the next interrogation?

Humor in the Short Stories: The Double-Sided Assemblage

In each of the short stories, humor emerges from the juxtaposition of two aspects of the assemblage: 1) "a machine assemblage of bodies, of actions and passions;" and 2) "a collective assemblage of enunciation of acts and statements, of incorporeal transformations attributed to bodies." (*A Thousand Plateaus* 88) Examples of the first include various machines: the ship machine, the hotel machine, the castle machine. (88) Examples of the second include "the regime of signs enunciation . . . each with its incorporeal transformations, acts, death sentences and judgments, proceedings, 'law.'" (88) The two sides can be seen in the instrument of torture and execution in "In the Penal Colony." The first side is seen in the physicality of the three-part contraption consisting of the bed, the Harrow, and the Designer. The second side is constituted by the exacting of justice upon the body of the prisoner: the machine literally inscribes the punishment onto the prisoner's body. Humor in this story is found in descriptions such as the following:

> in any case, the condemned man looked so like a submissive dog that one might have thought he could be left free to run on the surrounding hills and would only need to be whistled for when the execution was due to begin. (191)

However, the reader may respond with both contempt and sympathy for this dog-like condemned man. One can only wonder about what kind of a culture produces such behavior in its citizens. Another example of humor also contains exaggerations and social critique. The officer in charge of the apparatus declares: "My guiding principle is this: guilt is never to be doubted." (198)

In "The Judgment," the two sides of the assemblage are 1) the fiancée and the friend; and 2) being driven to suicide by his father for wanting to get married. The first is the desiring machine, the second the regime of signs, in this case, a death sentence pronounced by the father, to be carried out on himself. In this story, death has nothing to do with freedom; in fact, it is because the protagonist is unable to act independenly of his father's wishes that he dies. In "The Judgement," humor is found in the twisted, tortured relation between the father and the son. As Mark Anderson writes in his introduction to *The Sons*, "Despite its deadpan humor, this filial devotion had an extreme, even pathological quality . . . " (ix) Regarding this story, Kafka writes in his *Diaries* (1913):

> The friend is the strongest link between father and son, he is their strongest common bond. Sitting alone at his window, Georg rummages voluptuously in this consciousness of what they have in common, believes he has his father within him, and would be at peace with everything if it were not for a fleeting, sad thoughfulness. In the course of the story the father, with the strengthened position that the other, lesser things they share in common give him—love, devotion to the mother, loyalty to her memory, the clientele that he (the father) had been the first to acquire for the business—uses the common bond of the friend to set himself up as Georg's antagonist. Georg is left with nothing; the bride, who lives in the story only in relation to the friend, that is, to what father and son have in common, is easily driven away by the father since no marriage has yet taken place, and so she cannot penetrate the circle of blood relationship that is drawn around father and son. What they have in common is built up entirely around the father, Georg can feel it only as something foreign, something that has become independent, that he has never given enough protection, that is exposed to Russian revolutions, and only because he himself has lost everything except his awareness of the father does the judgement, which closes off his father from him completely, have so strong an effect on him. (215)

In this passage, we see the father as the side of the assemblage associated with the Law. Georg feels helplessly distanced from his father, and yet his "awareness of the father" is all that he has left in his life.

106   Kafka's Humor: The Castle Jester

In "The Judgment," the humor is sarcastic: the son calls his father a comedian. (60) When his father claims that the friend in St. Petersurg knows a thousand times better from the father's letters than the son's the details of the son's life, the son, attempting to make fun of his father, retorts "ten thousand times." (62) Georg's sarcastic humor is a nearly useless weapon the son half-heartedly hurls at his father; the irony of how ineffective Georg's sarcasm is signals the dismantling of the two sides of the machine; as Kafka writes in his diary, the bride exists only in relation to the friend, and by extension, to the father. Thus, the distinction son-desire-bride vs. father-Law is blurred.

In "The Metamorphosis," the two sides of the machine are: 1) the sister, the mother, and the woman in furs, which constitute the desiring machine, the machinic assemblage of bodies, action, and passions; and 2) being killed by the father, having been judged unfit to live after he refused to go to work. In this story, Deleuze and Guattari argue that Kafka's point is that it is better to die as a bug than to live as a bureaucrat. Again, this is not a Hegelian formulation about risking life by the bondsperson in order to take the place of the lord; rather, it is the rejection of a life diminished by the truncating effects of a bureaucracy and the Oedipal family structure. The extremely poignant and subtle humor in "The Metamorphosis" is found only in irony: for example, after Gregor dies, the family moves to a house they like better than the apartment they had before, "which Gregor had selected." (132)

In "Investigations of a Dog," the two sides of the assemblage are: 1) the dog-machine (the dog community), from which the narrator-dog becomes deterritorialized; and 2) the rules by which a dog must live in order to survive and the law of his dog ancestors, which possibly outlawed fasting. In "Investigations of a Dog," humor is found in relation to hunger: the narrator-dog tells us that at one point, he decides to fast until he can no longer stand it. With "hunger burning in [his] entrails," (308) he tried to imagine that he and hunger were separate and, as this task became more and more difficult, explained to himself: "'That is my hunger,' it was really my hunger that was speaking and having its joke at my expense." (309) This story is an inquiry into the scientific view of "the procuring of food:" on the one hand, "the actual preparation of the ground," and, on the other, "The auxialiry perfecting processes of incantation, dance, and song." (303) Kafka gives the example of "the scratching and watering of the ground" as a signifier linked to both the physical and the spiritual food of the dog.

In "A Hunger Artist," the two sides of the assemblage are: 1) the circus machine; and 2) the "sentence" of the hunger artist, that he die by starvation. The hunger artist confesses that he cannot control his refusal to eat because he cannot find the food that he likes. In his view, this invalidates him as a true hunger artist, and he did not deserve admiration. It is hard to justify a Hegelian reading that there is freedom in death. If anything, the hunger artist is addicted to starving himself. That this becomes a way to make a living is not an endorsement of Hegel but an indictment of a culture that rewards such an occupation, and even worse, at a certain point, loses interest in the occupation. In "A Hunger Artist," humor is found in ironic reversal: the hunger artist's happiest moment is in the morning, after a night of fasting, when the onlookers are fed breakfast, at his expense.

In "The Great Wall of China," the two sides of the assemblage are: 1) the wall machine, an assemblage of bodies and action, which delineates the boundaries of the Empire and which contains gaps; and 2) the law of the Empire, inaccessible to the common person. The narrator states that in some villages, even the name of the current dynasty is not known for certain. These two assemblages are dismantled in Kafka's humor. In this story humor is found in the irony that— analogous to the situation of verifying whether or not the narrator has actually eaten during his hunger strike in "The

Hunger Artist" — no one person can verify which gaps in the wall have been filled in because, "on acount of the extent of the structure," "no single man with his own eyes and judgment" can be certain of the extent of the entire structure." (235)

In "The Bucket Rider," the two sides of the assemblage collide when the "law" demands that the bucket rider must pay for the coal. The machine is the coal-bucket machine. Because the bucket rider cannot pay, he dies. Here humor is found in the absurdity of the bucket rider himself.

Humor in the Novels: Jus *and* Lex *for the Deterritorialized Worker and Kafka's Legacy*

In *Amerika, The Castle,* and *The Trial,* we find a relation between the forces of the desiring machine and the collective regime of signs. I will begin with one chapter of *Amerika,* "The Stoker." The desiring machine is the boiler room. What deterritorialized or brought Karl to the ship and the boiler room was his seduction by a young servant girl; that is, the connection to the machine is permeated with desire. The two sides of the assemblage are: 1) the boiler-room machine; and 2) the law of the sea — the sea captain's judgment reigning over all employees on the ship. The stoker is deterritorialized as a German in the United States (or at least a ship on its way to the U.S.). If he were living in Germany, his country of origin, he believes he would not have a Romanian boss. The stoker finds it intolerable to be given orders by a Romanian, whom he perceives to be his social inferior; he believes that Schubal favors foreigners (presumably, non-Germans). The stoker feels powerless in legal terms. Humor, if it may be called that, in "The Stoker" is found in the cruel treatment of the stoker; his plight is visible and important only to Karl. The senator, his shipmates, the captain, and the purser all see the stoker as a nuisance. Under these circumstances, how is he to find justice? This is the dilemma Lyotard decribes in *The Differend*: the gap between *jus* and *lex*.

In *The Castle*, one aspect of the assemblage consists of "the machinic assemblage of bodies, of actions and passions." Lust links K. and Freida, Frieda and Klamm, and a variety of women to the Castle; the other aspect of the assemblage, the "law," consists of the arbitrary, senseless, and total power over its subjects of the castle. This side of the assemblage is "a collective assemblage of enunciation of acts and statements of incorporeal transformations attributed to bodies." The women try to gain power for themselves and their families by using their sexuality. It is their endless desire to shorten the distance between themselves and the Castle that is pathetic and humorous, as is their contempt for "the peasants," to whom despite their status as prostitutes they feel superior, as well as their sycophantic relationship to officials of the Castle.

In *The Trial*, the machine consists of servant girls and maids; the "law" consists of the arbitrary power of the Court. K. is implicated and assigned responsibility in a variety of ways in the novel. He himself participates in a bureaucracy and a hierarchy at the bank; he follows its rules, including those of speaking down to his "inferiors." In his introduction to the Schocken edition of *The Trial*, George Steiner writes that Kafka's meditation on the law is related to Talmudic questioning: "it is the original mystery and subsequent applications of the law, of legalism and judgement which are the essential concern of Talmudic questioning. If, in the Judaic perception, the language of the Adamic was that of love, the grammars of fallen man are those of the legal code" (ix) He concludes that for Kafka, the definition of human life could be approximated as the freedom to be culpable, which is that of the fallen man. (xxi) Rather than speaking in theological terms, as relevant as they are in Kafka's case, I want to extend Steiner's insight to the broader philosophical and political implications that Antonio Negri puts forward in his book on Spinoza, *The Savage Anomaly*. According to Negri, we constitute the forces which we call "the state." Steiner also writes, correctly in my view, of the "kabbalistic geometries of ordered constructs with several centers" and these geometries inform *The Trial* (ix). Politically, it is by showing the multiple centers that a Deleuzian micropolitics is suggested. If there are many centers, then there are many ways to overcome the state(s). These strategies involve attention to how one is linked to the juridical and familial triangles through desire as well as to politcal analysis.

Steiner also points out that Milena and two of Kafka's sisters died in the holocaust. In a Latin American context, the example of Argentina's "dirty war" of the 1970s resonates in the arrests without stated charges in *The Trial*. Although most of the torture is psychological, until K. is finally killed, the human rights issues raised by *The Trial* are relevant today in relation to Mexico, even though human rights abuses there are not as well documented as in the Argentine case. Exaggerated political humor, a "minor genre" in Deleuze and Guattari's sense, particularly in relation to tragedy, continues to be a way for writers to circumvent censorship. Two examples are *Cola de Lagartija*, by Argentine writer Luisa Valenzuela, and *Haroun* (a children's book, an even more "minor" literature), by the British novelist of Indian descent, born in Bombay, Salman Rushdie. Even the right-wing Argentine writer Jorge Luis Borges, despite his own political views, becomes a critic of his authoritarian culture by merely describing it well, and in a Kafkaesque manner. Argentine writer Julio Cortázar's stories, particularly "Casa tomada" and "Apocalípsis at Solentiname," also share a debt to Kafka's legacy.

Humor, in *The Trial*, takes the form of exaggeration—to the point of absurdity—of the arbitrariness of the bureaucracy, of the ingratiating grovelling at the feet of those K. thinks may help him, and of his pathetic attempts to stay one step ahead of his persecutors and to maintain dignity. Humor is also linked to the dismantling of machines. For example, the lawyer is revealed to be the enemy, not the helper.

Conclusion

I have argued that a Deleuzo-Guattarian approach can help us to understand Kafka's humor as: 1) not funny (in a traditional sense); 2) social critique; and 3) linked to childhood experience. We have seen in the novels and a variety of short stories that Kafka's writing functions to "translate" social relations, including those of desire and the juridical, into assemblages. Somehow, often through a young woman, the protagonist is deterritorialized. In a vulnerable state, he usually finds that either he has been charged with a crime or forced to witness unjust treatment of someone else and is not able to do anything about it. The arbitrariness and "injustice" of the "punishment" never fit the crime, and yet the "punishment" is accepted. Humor is generated by the narrator's deadpan delivery of each of the incidents of "injustice." Humor dismantles the assemblages, revealing their component parts as tyrannical, unjust, arbitrary, and so on. We find Kafka's relentless social critique in this dismantling of the assemblages, that is, of the apparent social order, so as to reveal facets that have been hitherto underemphasized or less visible. Yet his critique of the state, of bureaucracies, and of the Oedipal structure is not stated. This remains the unuttered cry of a confused child who does not understand what justification there could possibly be for the severity of his punishment. We hear it in the silences.

Kafka's legacy lives on in the work of many contemporary writers, some of whose countries have suffered authoritarian regimes similar to those he described. These authors, including Cortázar and Valenzuela, have also used humor as a way to criticize repressive governments. While the term "Kafkaesque" has often been employed as a synonym for existential *angst*, for many Latin American writers the political context has been foregrounded.

Although it might at first appear that Kafka sees death as the only escape, he even dismantles the opposition life/

death; as Deleuze and Guattari put it, for Kafka, it is better to die as a bug than to live as a bureaucrat. Yet this is a philosophy of hope (if not for us). The "cure" for our sick, totalitarian, bureaucratic culture consists of the dismantling of the assemblages and overcoming of the sad passions, often linked to childhood trauma. As in *Don Quijote* a person who would attempt to create a good city as an alternative would have to be crazy, but only a crazy person would have the vision to make the attempt. The absence in Kafka's text, the good city, would not oppress its citizens as do the Court, the Castle, the Boiler Room, the Hotel. Rather, it would engender pleasant encounters. In this good city, differences could coexist, emotional paralysis could be overcome, and citizens would exist with the knowledge that Power was fully constituted by the multitude. Neither in the Hegelian state nor in death would the citizen find freedom; rather, freedom could be exercised by the affirmation of life, in everyday life, in a democracy. Both Kafka and Marx use irony in the context of serious political analysis. Whereas Marx foregrounded the worker, who was a citizen, in his analysis of capitalism, Kafka begins his analysis with the marginal, undocumented work, the deterritorialized border dweller.

Note

[1]George Steiner, "Introduction," Franz Kafka, *The Trial*, xii. Steiner writes: "Reading the blackest of modern myths, "The Metamorphosis," to a circle of aghast intimates, Kafka himself doubled over with laughter." (xvi) John Updike, in his foreword to *The Complete Stories*, writes; "The charm that these disquieting, abortive early pieces exerted upon Brod and other authors (for Kafka used to read his work aloud to friends, sometimes laughing so hard he could not continue reading) must have largely derived the the quality of their German prose." (xiii)

Works Cited

Anderson, Mark. "Introduction," Franz Kafka, *The Sons*. New York: Schocken, 1989.

Deleuze, Gilles and Felix Guattari. *A Thousand Plateaus, Capitalism and Schizophrenia*. Minneapolis: University of Minnesota Press, 1987.

_____. *Kafka, Toward a Minor Literature*. Trans. Dana Polan. Minneapolis and London: University of Minnesota Press, 1986.

Freud, Sigmund. "The Uncanny." *The Standard Edition of the Complete Psychological Works of Freud*. Ed. James Strachey, in coll. with Anna Freud, ass. by Alix Strachey and Alan Tyson. London: International Psycho-Analytical Press. 17. 219.

Kafka, Franz. "The Metamorphosis," in *The Penal Colony and Other Stories*. Trans. Willa and Edwin Muir. 1945. New York: Schocken, 1995.

_____. *The Castle*. Trans. Willa and Edwin Muir with add. material trans. by Eithne Wilkins and Ernst Kaiser. Rpt. New York: Penguin, 1971.

_____. *The Complete Stories*. New York: Schocken, 1971.

_____. *The Sons*. New York: Schocken, 1989.

_____. *The Trial*. Intro. George Steiner. Trans. Willa and Edwin Muir. Rev. and with add. material trans. E. M. Butler. New York: Schocken, 1976.

_____. *The Blue Octavo Notebooks*. Ed. Max Brod, trans. Ernst Kaiser and Eithne Wilkins. Cambridge: Exact Change, 1991.

Lacan, Jacques. "Tuché and Automaton." *The Four Fundamental Concepts of Psychoanalysis*. Ed. Jacques-Alain Miller. Trans. Alan Sheridan. New York: Norton, 1978.

Miller, Alice. *The Untouched Key*. New York: Anchor Books, 1990.

Negri, Tony. *The Savage Anomaly*. Trans. Michael Hardt. Minneapolis: University of Minnesota Press, 1991.

Spinoza, Baruch. Ethics, *Treatise on the Emendation of the Intellect and Selected Letters*. Trans. Samuel Shirley. Ed. and introd. by Seymour Feldman. Indianapolis: Hackett, 1992.

Steiner, George. "Introduction," Franz Kafka. *The Trial*. Trans. Willa and Edwin Muir. Rev. and with add. material E. M. Butler. New York: Schocken, 1976.

CONTRIBUTORS

Augusto Monterroso
Born in 1921 in Guatemala, Monterroso has lived in exile in Mexico since 1944. In 1975 he received the Villaurrutia prize in honor of his international stature as a writer. In 1988 he was awarded the prestigious "Aztec Eagle." Named "Man of the Year in Literature" by Cambio 16 of Madrid in 1994, Monterroso was feted throughout the world with literary prizes and recognition. His books have earned him universal acclaim by the intellectual and literary communities of our times. The author has been translated into almost every language, including English, French, Chinese, Swedish, and Latin. Among his works, which include narrative and essays, are *Obras Completas y Otros Cuentos* (1959), *La Oveja Negra y Demás Fábulas* (1969), *Movimeinto Perpetuo* (1972), *Lo Demás Es Silencio* (1978), *Viaje al Centro de la Fábula* (1981), *La Palabra Mágica* (1983), *La Letra E* (1987), and most recently *Los Buscadores de Oro* (1995).

Héctor Ortega
He began his theatrical activities in the theater group of the Faculty of Architecture of UNAM; studied theater, pantomime, and dance in the "Theater Studio" workshops, with instructors such as Alejandro Jodorowsky, Carlos Ancira, Guillermo Arriaga, Juan José Arreola; created the "First Company of Mimes of Mexico" with Alejandro Jodorowsky; as actor, received numerous prizes after that received from the Association of Theater Critics of the Mexican Republic to the "Theatrical Revelation" in 1960; as a director, actor, and screenwriter, and playwright, has received three Ariels, two Silver Goddesses, The Herald; first National Prize in the screenplay competition of the General Society Mexican Writers for his screenplay *Cuartelazo*; best comedy actor in 1985 for

The Accidental Death of an Anarchist; considered by the press as one of the best Latin American actors at the Festival of Manizales in Colombia and Cordoba in Argentina; representing Mexico, attended the Festival of the Nations in Paris, France; in 1988 received the Ariel for the best supporting actor for his presentation in the movie *Mariana, Mariana;* during 1988 and 1989 made five movies as an actor and was nominated for the Ariel as "best supporting actor" for his performance in the film *The Cost of* Life; in 1990 received by unanimous jury vote the scholarship of the Bank of Screenplays of the Section of Authors of the Union of Cinematography Production for the writing of his script *Macho Word;* wrote and directed for the television program "Les Gourmetes" *The Marked Hour.*

Manuel Flores

Born in Mexico in 1959, Flores studied at the State University of Education. Early on he experienced the life of the art and cultural community of Mexico City where he was involved in the performing arts with such renowned figures as Héctor Ortega, José Luis Cuevas, and Rafael Elizondo. In Hollywood, California, Flores studied scene breakdown at UCLA and was affiliated with the Bilingual Foundation of the Arts under the direction of Carmen Zapata and Margarita Galván. He has been active as an experimental videomaker, playwright, and author of screenplays for motion pictures. Flores has published short stories, essays, and film criticism.

Hugo Hiriart

Born in Mexico in 1942, Hiriart studied philosophy at the National Autonomous University of Mexico. Thanks to a fellowship from the Guggenheim Foundation, he was able to move to Spain in 1985. In Washington, D.C., Hiriart wrote fiction at the Woodrow Wilson Center for Foreign Scholars. He currently resides in Mexico, where he is a playwright and stage director. Hiriart's widely acclaimed publications include *Disertación Sobre las Telarañas* (1980), *La Destrucción de Todas las Cosas* (1992), *Galaor,* and *Cuadernos de Gofa*. He has written short stories for children as well as essays and numerous plays.

D. Emily Hicks

Author of *Border Writing: The Multimensional Text* (Minnesota, 1991), D. Emily Hicks is a critic and performance artist active in border culture. Her articles include "Boundaries To Which One Is Tied And From Which One Is Restrained From Traversing" (the central work in the catalogue which accompanied *Counterweight: Alienation, Assimilation, Resistance,* an exhibition at the Santa Barbara Contemporary Arts Forum (Nov., 1992-Jan., 1993) and "Border Peformance Texts" (published in *RLA)*. Her *Nietzsche and Performance* is currently under consideration at Minnesota, as is *Border Culture: Art and Theory,* coedited with William A. Nericcio and Harry Polkinhorn.

José Luis Cuevas

Born in Mexico City in 1934, Cuevas is an engraver, draughtsman, painter, sculptor, stage designer, and internationally renowned illustrator and author. He has been honored with numerous prizes throughout the world and is considered one of Mexico's most important living cultural figures. His books include *Cuevario* (1973), *En Torno a Cuevas* (1985), *Cuevas antes de Cuevas* (1990), *Gato Macho* (1994), and *Municiones de Caviar: Poemas a José Luis Cuevas* (1995). In his column "Cuevario," Cuevas is a regular contributor to the cultural supplement "El Búho" of Mexico City's prestigious *Excélsior* newspaper.

Figure 9. "Judge of instruction." José Luis Cuevas. 1982.

Figure 10. "Office manager." José Luis Cuevas. 1982.

Figure 11. "Kullisch." José Luis Cuevas. 1982.

Figure 12. "Martyr with impaled hands." José Luis Cuevas. 1982.

Figure 13. "Martyr looking up at an angel looking down from a hole in the sky." José Luis Cuevas. 1982.

Figure 14. "The lawyer." José Luis Cuevas. 1982.

Figure 15. Stage setting for original production.

Figure 16. "I'd rather wait for your superior officer."

Figure 17. "K. decided to go straight home."

Figure 18. "Miss Bürstner, I'd very much like to call you by your first name."

Figure 19. "I see him down flat on the floor, surrounded by splashes of blood."

Figure 20. "The farther in I go, the worse I feel."

Figure 21. "I just broke a plate against the wall to make you come."

Figure 22. "Well, if you're innocent, the problem is very simple. But . . . are you innocent?"

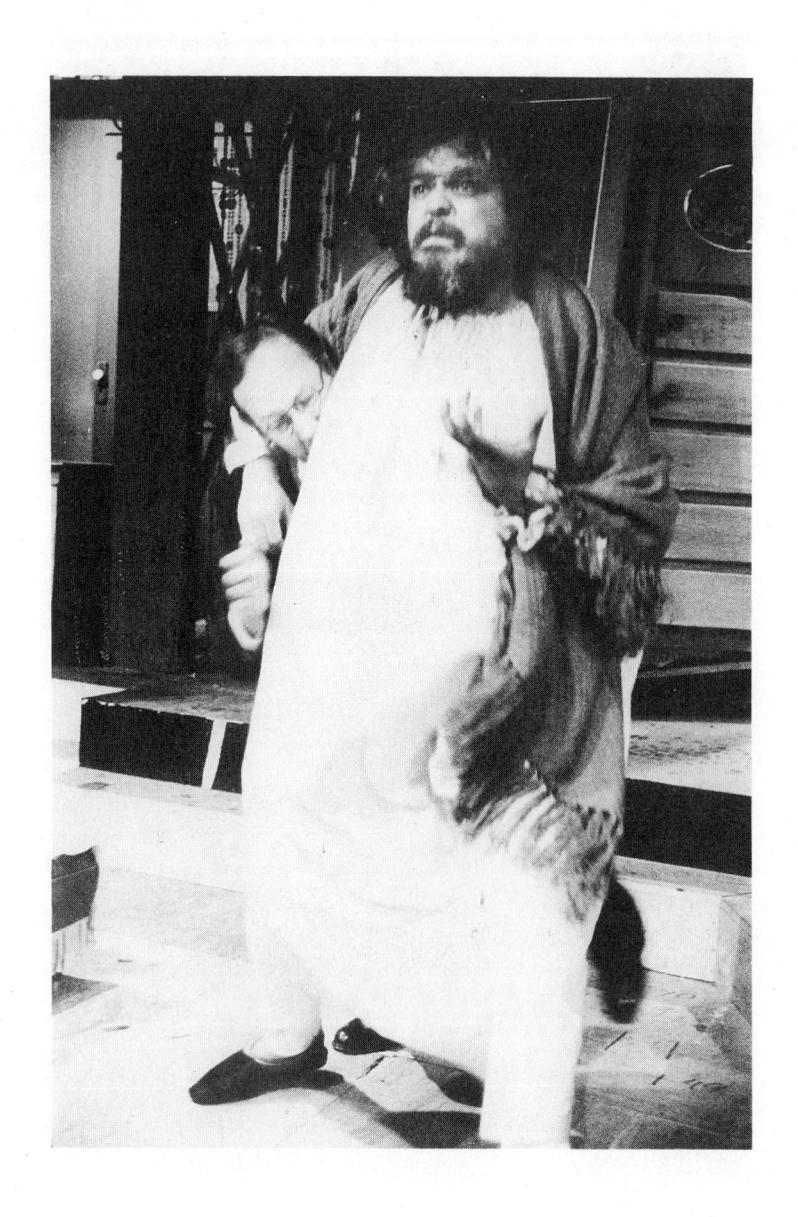

Figure 23. "Your bad opinion about the way I have conducted myself is because of the soft way you have been treated."

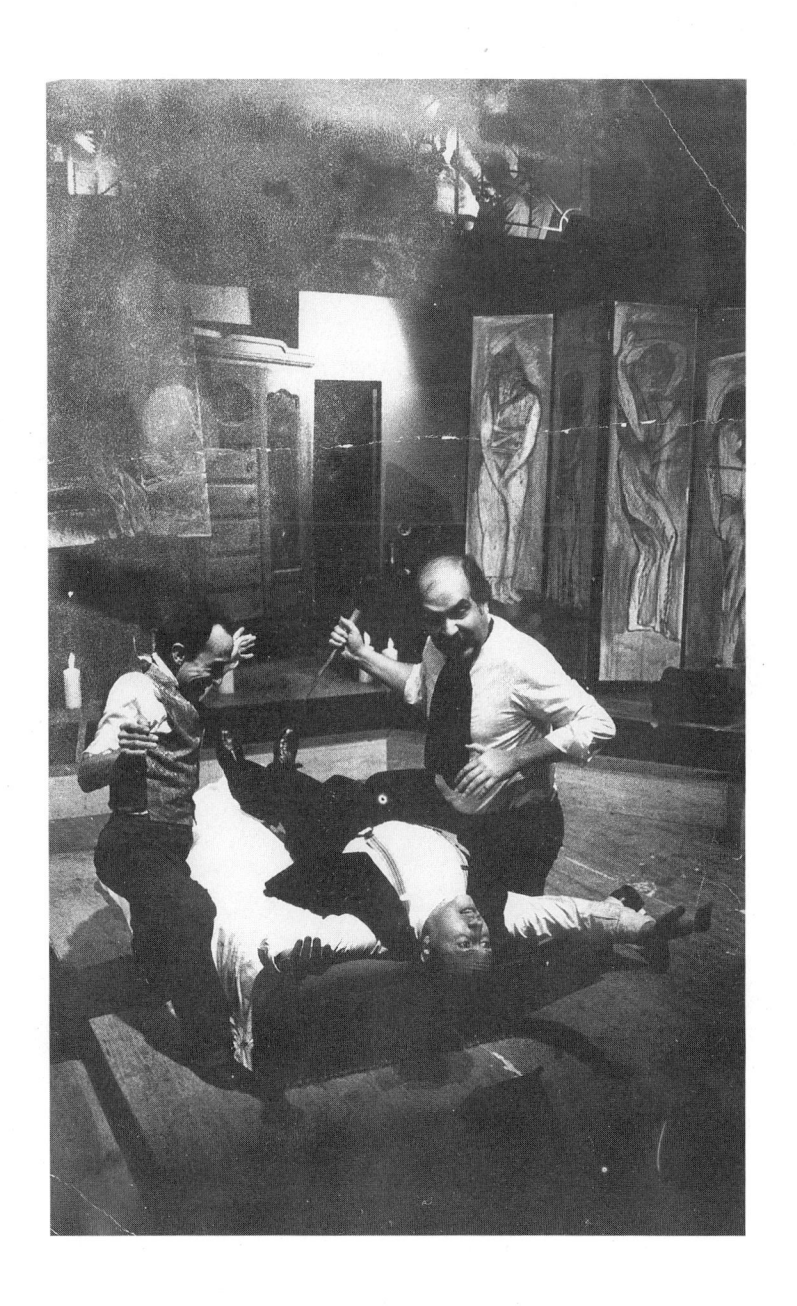

Figure 24. "'Like a dog!' said K., before he died."

Figure 25. Héctor Ortega, José Luis Cuevas, Ricardo Díaz Muñoz, Rafael Elizondo, Manuel Flores. Opening night, June, 1982.

Figure 26. "That's enough for today; so, we can say good-bye, for now, of course."

Printed Fall 1996 in Wisconsin
for San Diego State University Press
by Remembrance Publications,
this edition of
*The Comic Trial of Joseph K.:
Text & Context*
was set in Book Antigua 11
and is limited to 500 copies
bound in wrappers.

¥

Cueva 1982

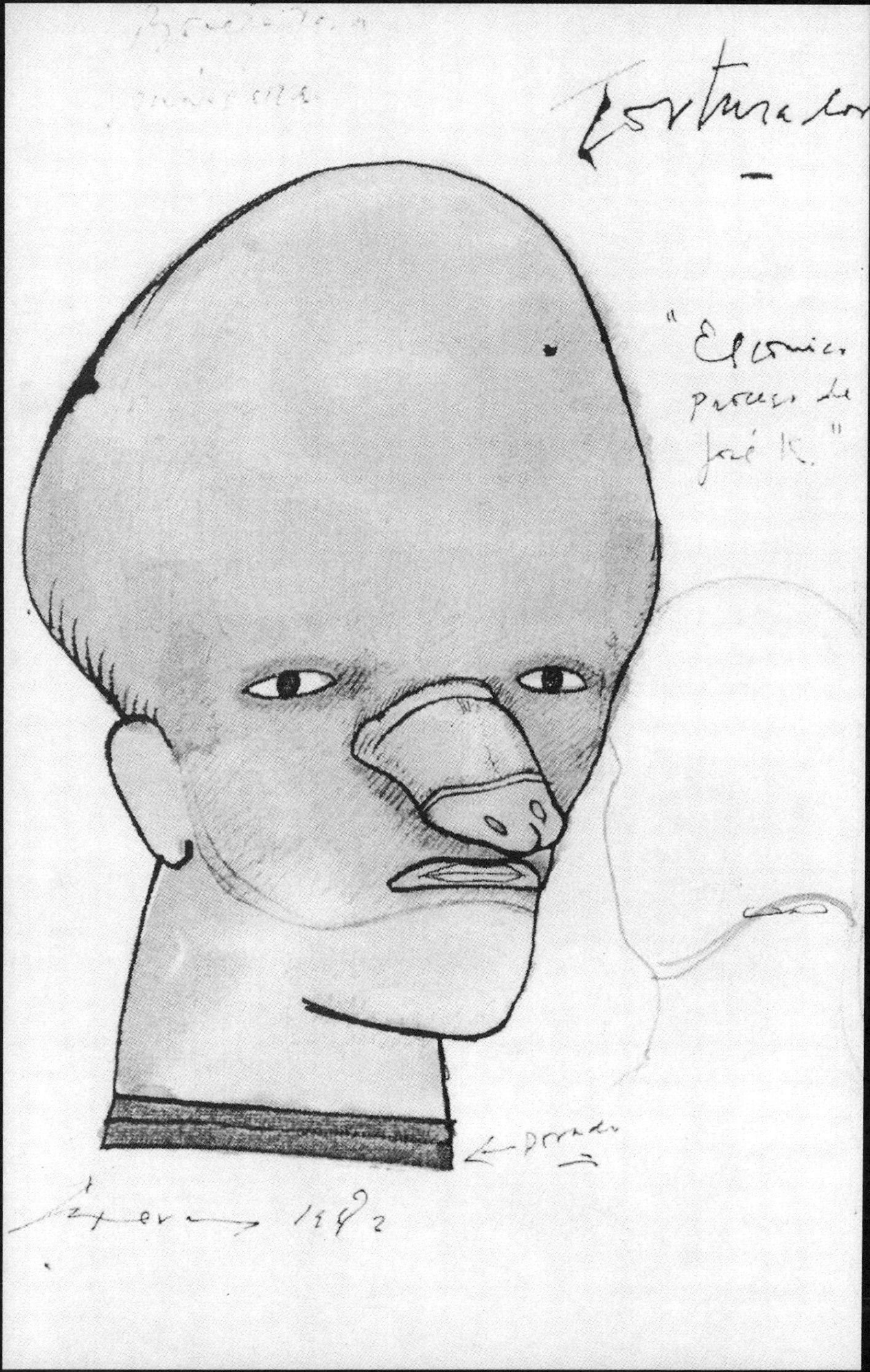
Torturador
"El cómico proceso de José K."